MORE (
PETER GIRARD'S
GUERNSEY

MORE OF
PETER GIRARD'S
GUERNSEY

A SECOND MISCELLANY OF GUERNSEY'S
HISTORY AND ITS PEOPLE

Peter J. Girard

MORE OF PETER GIRARD'S GUERNSEY
A Second Miscellany of Guernsey's History and its People

ISBN 0 902550 42 X

First published in Great Britain 1990

Copyright © Peter J. Girard

Published by The Guernsey Press Company Ltd,
Braye Road, Vale, Guernsey, Channel Islands.

This book is set in 10/11 pt Baskerville Medium.

Made and printed by The Guernsey Press Company Ltd,
Braye Road, Vale, Guernsey, Channel Islands.

CONTENTS

		Page
1.	Changes through the ages	11
2.	A hill that captured the imagination of the people	19
3.	Sand along our coasts	24
4.	La Mare de Carteret	29
5.	Farmers and Cattle	33
6.	The Song of the Landsman (poem in Guernsey French, translated into English and written by Mr T. Lenfestey)	39
7.	Le Moulin de Haut	41
8.	Lihou Island	47
9.	The Magic Well	53
10.	Mysterious wrecking — the *Briseis*	56
11.	Le Grand Havre — Le Braye du Valle, fishing boats, wrecks and a whale	61
12.	The Privateering Era	69
13.	A Close Shave	78
14.	The Vazon Story Teller	81
15.	Horsy Tales	88
16.	My Aunt (Portions of Poems written in Guernsey French by Georges Metivier)	93
17.	For Pions a kiss for every girl they met	96
18.	More reminiscences of R. O. Falla, O.B.E.	102
19.	Admiral The Rt Hon. James Lord de Saumarez, G.C.B., K.S., General of Marines, 1757-1836	109
20.	Lieutenant-General Sir John Doyle, Baronet, G.C.B., K.C.	124
21.	Major-General Sir Isaac Brock, K.B.	129
22.	Lieutenant George Edward Nurse, V.C. A valiant resident of the Castel Parish	137
23.	Lavoirs still used by French women	144
24.	Castle Cornet at War. Escape in the nick of time	148
25.	The Church in Guernsey at the Reformation	151
26.	The Castel School	155
27.	Guernsey families take refuge in America	161
28.	St Germain Quarry (Golden Gravel as used by the Gentry)	165
29.	Stories of the little people told around the Terpi	170
30.	Cobo Soup Kitchen	176
31.	The Fate of Our Old Batteries	182
32.	Problems of a Couple in the Autumn of their Lives	187
33.	National Trust Property	191
34.	A place for marvelling at Cobo sunsets	196
35.	Christmas Festivities during the Occupation	201
36.	We will go no more to sea (Poem written in Guernsey French by Georges Metivier translated into English)	205
37.	Local terminology involving land and local administration	209

ACKNOWLEDGEMENTS

I wish to record the following names of those who so willingly
helped me to compile this book.

P. J. Girard

Mrs M. Austin
Mr David Bedford
Mr George Bramall
Mr R. O. Falla. O.B.E.
Mr Basil Gaudion
Mr Basil Girard
The Staff of the Greffe Office
Mr W. H. Girard (Ontario)
Mr M. J. Gaudion
Mr Arthur Klein
Mr J. H. Lenfesty
Miss D. White
Miss Rosalyn McClean
Mr L. James Marr
Mr T. F. Priaulx
Mrs P. Ryan
Mr P. M. Sarl
The Rev. Michael Star
The Director and Staff of Priaulx Library
Royal Guernsey Agricultural & Horticultural Society
Mr C. R. Sackett
Captain Philip Saumarez, D.S.C., R.N. (Rtd)
Mr Dan Savident
Mr W. F. Tipping
Mr Carel Toms
Miss L. P. Vessey
Mr Bertie Wright

FOREWORD

By Raymond Falla, O.B.E.

IN this book Peter Girard has chronicled in a fascinating way events, sayings, records, etc., and described personalities in an interesting manner.

In my view it is a must for every Guernsey-born person and visitor to read and I feel that it should be available to schools and to other educational institutions.

In Guernsey so little is known about the past and of our heritage which should be incumbent upon every Guernsey-born person to cherish and preserve.

In the past Guernsey people have produced a considerable number of "raconteurs" (story-tellers) such as Georges Metivier, Denis Corbet, Tom Lenfesty and Tom Mahy — all whose poetry is worth recording as has been done in this book.

Finally I consider this to be most readable and I recommend it to all who love to read a good book.

October, 1990.

PREFACE

DISCOVERING that my previous book published in 1986 and called *Peter Girard's Guernsey* had been well received I decided to spend some of the unpleasant winter days in writing a second book.

As in the case of the first book I used some articles of mine which had been printed in the *Guernsey Evening Press*, but I was also faced with the prospect of finding suitable subjects to fill the remainder of the book.

I was indeed very fortunate in receiving very considerable help from Chris Sackett, managing director of the Guernsey Press Company, as well as from other well known personalities such as Carel Toms, R. O. Falla, O.B.E., Captain Philip Saumarez, D.S.C., R.N. (Rtd), Dr Harry Tomlinson, F. H. Lenfestey, Arthur Klein, Basil Gaudion, Basil Girard, James Marr and George Bramall. I must also mention my typist, Rosalyn McClean, for the excellent work she produced.

For the second time, I write in the hope that a substantial number of people will be interested in reading tales of ancient Guernsey as well as those of more recent times. In addition, I hope that the records of the lives of some great Guernseymen will be read with interest. These include Rt Hon. James Lord de Saumarez, G.C.B., K.S., Lieut-General Sir John Doyle, Baronet, G.C.B., K.C., and Major-General Sir Isaac Brock, K.B. The adventures of Lieut. George Edward Nurse, V.C., should also help to produce a feeling of wonder that such a keen fighting man lived through so many dangers.

Some of my tales are also meant to produce laughter and some deal with the way we overcame many of the trials of the Occupation period. The inclusion of some Guernsey French poems (with translations) should provide interest and amusement.

Finally, I can state that the book is suitable for young and old alike who are interested in the development of our Island Home.

P. J. Girard
October 1990

To my grandchildren

Changes through the ages in the system of land holding in Guernsey

IT is generally accepted that the first cultivators of land were the Mesolithic settlers who lived at the period when hunting and fishing were not considered sufficient to maintain a considerable population.

It is felt that Guernsey, in all probability, was colonised by sea at the end of the first wave of human movement passing across Western Europe from the East around 6,500 years ago. One can but admire settlers for their courage in crossing the Channel in primitive craft often bringing with them not only the seeds of the domestic crops of those days but also animal breeding stocks.

At that time the homes such as they were, would have been built not far from mysterious chambered tombs and not far from the sea so that the inhabitants could fish and gather the edible products to be found on the sea shore.

It would appear that the first cultivation was carried out on land now generally covered by sand and it is obvious that at first the "slash and burn" technique must have been used to clear land for farming and to provide fresh areas as the soil in use became exhausted. There is little doubt that during the years which were ahead of the settlers there was a continual rise in the level of the sea, which has again risen some 10 metres in the last few thousand years and is still continuing a definite rise. Thus a very large area of Guernsey is lost possibly for ever. Another factor which was clearly shown in the Cobo Long House dig was the vast amount of sand blown at intervals from the sea shore, making cultivation impossible as well as ruining living conditions.

A third factor which caused movement inland of the inhabitants was the exposed nature of the coastal site, making it subject not only to the bad weather conditions already mentioned but also to possible attacks by bands of invaders.

The gradual movement inland of farmers and their stock was made directly into valleys where shelter, water and possible protection from enemies made this a very wise move.

Once established they began to cultivate whatever land was available but soon they discovered that in order to grow good crops on the slopes of valleys it was necessary to form terraces.

However, as time went on and the population increased it became absolutely necessary to venture into the uplands where large clearings made by communal effort could be shared out between those involved. Remains of this cultivation can be found in the form of the polished stone axe-heads which they used as tools.

The farmers had cattle, goats, pigs, sheep, dogs and in their fields they raised oats, barley, peas, beans and lentils but few root crops. These crops were probably manured with animal manure and seaweed. In time the people were guided by leaders who must have been well acquainted with the "Open Field" system of agriculture in which the shares made took the form of strips (which in Guernsey were called "Camps"). Thus people who had built up a nucleated village had their "Camps" in the nearest "Open Field".

The strips or "Camps" were separated from one another

Strip Farming at Pleinmont.

12

by baulks of soil some of which are still visible in the "Open Field" on the flat top of Pleinmont where some of the original "Camps" can also be seen.

The Fief system introduced by the Normans no doubt reinforced the "Open Field" system by bringing discipline which in spite of demanding dues and services assured the holders of a considerable security of tenure. However at the same time the tenants contributed liberally to the comforts and well being of the "Seigneurs" or Lords of the Manors. The Seigneurs were also subject to the Ceremony of Homage to the reigning Monarch in his or her capacity as successors to the Dukes of Normandy. On such special occasions the Seigneurs were expected to demonstrate their loyalty in a ceremonial manner, this being a reminder of the early days when Seigneurs who fell out of favour could be deprived of the considerable benefits attached to their position as Seigneur and actually the loss of a Fief could occur for purely political reasons.

In early days "Fiefs" amounted to large areas of land which were granted to noble Lords and to French Abbeys and it would appear that monks attached to the Abbey of Mont St Michel, which had been granted a Fief in Guernsey, were extremely helpful as they taught farmers how to improve the working land, the care of animals and the clearing of waste land. Of course the results of their endeavours were such as to increase the dues to be collected by their Seigneur. There is little doubt that the example set by these monks was copied by others and so their efforts had an Island-wide effect.

Thus the extent of the cultivable land was increased over a very wide area as was the common land available for grazing of animals. Any new cultivable land could be used to increase the number of "Camps" available for farmers who were anxious to grow suitable crops during the period of "Mession" when cattle and sheep were hobbled and kept away from the Open fields used by the Farmers.

Freedom for the animals was restored when all the crops had been gathered in by the farmers and the period of "Banon" was in force. Banon was merely the name given to the opening of the cultivated fields to animals who could graze over the Camps and eat every morsel of suitable food left on the land. This period lasted approximately from

13

From the air a portion of the Castel showing small fields often of irregular shapes.

September to March and after this period Mession was pronounced when all fields were closed and used for the owners own purposes.

It was not until 1717 that the Banon was brought to an end and animals were no longer allowed to wander freely over the stubble during the period of Banon.

As enclosures were being made with hedges which were usually massive earth banks, the animals belonging to the prosperous farmers benefitted whereas there were animals belonging to the less prosperous which at times had to content themselves with grazing in the grassy lanes.

The sixteenth and the first half of the seventeenth century were periods of very active hedge building but unfortunately for the cottagers the parish commons and waste lands were not spared. In fact it has been reported that Queen Elizabeth's commissioners bought most of these areas at a very low rate. However it appears that a group of men who had formerly used the commons went to the places where they had once existed and broke down the enclosures. After this the Commissioners of the Commonwealth recommended that the commons should be restored to the people and that under the supervision of officers of every parish they should be let for a yearly rental to tenants who could improve them and that the rents should be used for the benefit of the poor.

Unfortunately nothing seems to have been carried out and this remained as a bone of contention between the parochial authorities and the Privy Council.

Mr J. H. Lenfestey, Archivist, found that in 1470 the land was divided into camps, pieches, etc and one occasional courtil and clos (Enclosures). By 1548 some consolidation of camps had taken place, this involving the uniting of two or more camps and pieches to form larger areas of land.

The introduction of the word "pieche" needs explanation. This merely involves areas of land of an indefinite size used for normal cropping even forming part of a camp.

By 1584 even more consolidation had occurred and by 1634 more Courtils (fields) appeared in the Livres de Perchage and some of the Courtils had camps and pieches enclosed within their boundaries which probably consisted of stout hedges. However, Mr Lenfestey reported that by 1662 a definite pattern of change could be recognised although remnants of the older system remained. Lastly it could be seen that by 1709 the present pattern was well established.

In continuing our consideration of the treatment of the land we find that the "Camps" or strips were eventually accompanied by "pieches" even in the remaining "Open fields". Actually in the early days of this century the farmers owning large fields often split them up into "pieches" each carrying a different crop. There crops could be corn, turnip, beetroot, cattle carrots, parsnips then eventually some kale, maize and vegetable crops such as potatoes, but nowadays these fields usually provide grass for the making of silage and little else is grown.

In considering the remnants remaining from the earliest days that we can find it is astonishing to discover that on the flat land on the upper areas of Pleinmont one can find the remains of the whole system of Camps or strips once owing homage to the Fief of Pleinmont.

Special seigneurial privileges included that of keeping 'Colombiers' or pigeon towers, whilst other gentlemen of standing owning smaller estates were allowed to build pigeon-holes below the eaves of the gable of a building.

Thus hundreds of pigeons were kept and they consumed large quantities of the tenants' grain which obviously caused grave losses.

Guernsey now has one 'Colombier' which can be seen at St Pierre du Bois and the base of another at Lihou Island.

The hunting of conies (as wild rabbits were called) was also restricted to the high ranking officials of the Island and they tended to confine their rabbits to warrens or 'Garennes'. As a result a considerable amount of poaching took place in spite of the extremely severe penalties in force, so that the tenants had to suffer from the extensive amount of damage done by the rabbits which managed to escape from the 'Garenne'.

Ploughing contest at Vimiera. Two shires pulling a modern plough.

In Guernsey we still have a 'Warren' but unfortunately it is practically ignored by the population and by visitors, partly because it is tucked away behind houses and other buildings in Rue de la Cache, St Sampson's. Few people realise that this 'Warren' dates back to 1261 and retains many features illustrating its ancient origin.

As a result of the general restrictions placed upon the lower classes robberies were common and the punishments were severe including imprisonment, whipping (24 lashes with blood running) and hanging.

Old fashioned churn.

17

As years passed by the production of cider became an important Island industry and farmers became interested in measures which would shelter the apple trees and other fruit crops so that the planting of elm trees on the hedges or near the hedges became important. Gorse was also planted on the hedges and provided the necessary heat for many of the Island ovens.

From very early days there were water mills in such suitable places as the Talbot Valley which no doubt were used to deal with corn brought to them by neighbouring farmers.

The earliest reliable date that I could locate for the Talbot Valley mills was one of 1331 when the water mills at L'Echelle were recorded as being the property of the Crown.

There were other mills owned by the Crown or by the Seigneurs of the Fiefs and in each case a miller was entrusted with the grinding of the corn which was grown in abundance in the Island. So much so that I discovered a record of 1238 in which by means of a Royal permit the Seigneur of the Fief Le Comte was allowed to export corn to ports in Normandy.

When extra labour was required in connection with the mills it would appear that in early days this was regarded as compulsory labour for the tenants by at least some of the Seigneurs.

By the 13th Century windmills were erected to supplement the existing watermills no doubt because at times of the year the water available to drive the mill became scarce. In the same way there were periods when the wind was absent and the attention of farmers was drawn to the use of the water mills.

A hill that captured the imagination of the people

FROM dim and distant past, the hill on which the Castel Church stands has drawn the attention of the inhabitants of the neighbourhood.

First of all, we must consider the Menhir or Grande Mère, that remarkable sculpture which was dug out of the church during renovations and now stands boldly to the north of the church door.

It is regarded as one of the finest in Europe and dated as 2500-1800 B.C. by Dr Ian Kinnes. For a long period, it has been associated with the cult of the mother goddess, but there is little doubt that it must have attracted and awed the population.

The next great change on this hill-top may well have been association with the Roman period, as we are assured that pieces of Roman tiling have been found in the masonry of the walls, while a curious structure found below the church floor appears to indicate Roman occupation of the site.

The Menhir at the Castel Church. From that point is a good view of the lower north of the island.

Following this period, there are very convincing traditions that renegade Vikings occupied the hill-top, building themselves as strong fortifications as they could. This, then, is the Châtel or Câtel from which the parish has derived its name, although I have an old document which refers to the Castel as the Parish of the Saracen.

The Grand Saracen was the leader of the band and there is little doubt that he and his followers filled the people with considerable fear.

The next adventure to overtake this hill resulted from the coming of Christianity to the island, following which churches were built in each of the parishes.

At first, there is little doubt that they were much smaller and less robust than at present.

However, the effect of the appearance of the Roman Catholic Church in the parish was to produce a slight change in its name to La Paroisse de Sainte Marie du Castro. Even then they could not keep the Saracen Castle out of the title.

Unfortunately, French raid after French raid left the churches in a very bad state and in some cases the rebuilding took years to complete and when rebuilt they were constructed in such a way as to act as places of refuge and defence as well as of worship.

So much of the social life of the parish was centred in the church that definite paths were recognised as church paths. They all led to the church, thus providing links with the distant parts of the parish, along which people went to church to baptise their little ones, to pray, to bury their dead and to witness the weddings of their children.

Along these paths were a number of crosses, healing wells and small chapels. In addition, it is very likely that they acted as sanctuary paths, along which a criminal who had put himself at the mercy of the Church, could eventually escape to the coast.

It has already been noted that the churches were regarded as places of refuge and defence and this belief is strengthened by the fact that they had butts close to the church, where it was customary to practise archery.

Thus we know that in 1569 the butts were in a bad way and the two parish constables, Guillome Ossene and Edouart Le Feywre, were ordered to repair them 'within a day' or be prepared to spend a sojourn in a suitable Castle Cornet dungeon.

In the same year, we can read in John Girard's diary that he had his 'haquebute' checked. This was a superior type of cross-bow. At the same time he sold a dirk to G. Marquis and bought what was no doubt a better one.

Another entry in the same diary records another occasion when John Girard again attended to his armaments.

He went to Town and bought a sword and a dagger, both of which he lent to someone taking part in a military review. In addition, someone else asked him for the loan of his haquebute and the appurtenances belonging to it.

It was not until towards the end of the 16th century that we read of guns and shot being used and the Militia had to wait until the end of the 18th century before the British Government provided the uniforms and accoutrements.

By the middle of the 18th century, conditions in France were causing alarm in the island and several parishes were provided with guns.

Thus in 1755 alterations were made to the doors of the Town Church to enable them to be used for the movement of the parish guns.

Similar provision had to be made at the Castel, while at St Saviour's the gun was housed in a separate addition in front of the church.

By 1793, the vicinity of the churchyard of the Castel could still provide enough space for the entire Militia to parade, where they were inspected by the Lieutenant-Governor, no doubt viewed by an admiring crowd. Indeed, the churchyard was the rallying point if any alarm was raised during the Republican and Napoleonic wars with France.

After considering some of the effects of the threat of war upon the 'environs' of the Church of the Castel we should now consider how the people received enjoyment from the same surroundings.

In order to do this we have to go back to the pre-Reformation days, when the fairs were wonderful occasions for all the population. They supplied all the attractions common to this period, including side shows, music, dances, refreshments and amusements — in fact all the 'fun of the fair', including buying and selling at stalls.

These fairs were usually held in connection with the celebration of Saints Days and we read that John Girard was a 'batonnier', no doubt heading processions and taking part in the special services in the church.

Of course all such 'superstitious' practices were stopped during the 100 years of Calvinism in Guernsey and one wonders how any of the old dances and customs were retained.

Eventually, as the centuries went by, changes took place in the composition of the fairs, the most important being the introduction of animals for sale and for exhibition.

In addition, the time came when only one big fair was held and this was at Michaelmas, possibly a connection with the enjoyments which long ago had accompanied the services involved in the day set apart for the celebration of Saint Michael and All Angels — a festival held at a time when the harvest was in and all were on a day's holiday.

In 1749, a bomb-shell affected those responsible for organising the fair, when it was known that the open, grassy, southern side of the churchyard was to be enclosed, so that although free of graves it would not be available for the fair. This enclosure made the roadway much too narrow to stage the fair.

Following this the States were asked to buy a suitable area in the vicinity of the church where the fair could be held.

Eventually, after much difficulty, a field was found which today is still known as The Fair Field and it was fitted with toilets, seating accommodation and suitable places to tie bulls, cows and other animals. The upright stones and the tethering chains which were fitted from one stone top to another, are still used, but at Saumarez Park, where they were taken some years ago.

However, it was not until 1817 that a Society of Agriculture was formed when it was formally decided that on the Friday before 'La St Jean' (Midsummer Day, 24 June) a fair would be held as well as on other occasions when and where a central committee should decide.

It appears that the first show of the Society was held on 25 June 1817 and in all probability it was held in the new Fair Field.

In 1823, a horse was imported which was described as a superb stallion named Cottager and in 1826 owners of colts sired by Cottager were invited to show them at the show, but after a short time, the Fair Field became too small to cope

22

with the number of people attending. Thus in 1882 the stallions and colts were displayed in a field belonging to Mr T. Lenfestey of Les Fontaines.

I well remember attending the show as a lad and spending most of my time in the large field at Les Touillets which was conveniently placed to the show ground. I remember watching 'skill driving' using ponies and traps and I do believe I saw the same competition being carried on with cars.

Now the Fair Field remains as a memorial to the great efforts made by our ancestors to improve the type of horned cattle and horses on the island and, incidentally, carrying on the tradition of a fair of medieval times.

Incidentally, the memorial in the middle of the field under the magnificent trees was erected to the memory of Mr Nicolas Le Beir for his devoted service over a long period to the Royal Guernsey Agricultural and Horticultural Society.

Fair Field (Castel) — bought by the States in mid 18th century. In centre is memorial to Mr Nicolas Le Beir for devoted service to Royal Guernsey Agricultural and Horticultural Society.

Sand along our coasts

RECENTLY I felt the urge to discover more facts concerning the how, when and where of dune formation and of the blowing sand. I found that the formation of coastal sand dunes and the blowing in of sand from the beaches is difficult to study because of the underlying causes interconnected with changes in the relative levels of land and sea and with changes temporary or long lasting in the climate of the region concerned.

Where there have been extensive expanses of dunes, much misery must have been caused due to the encroachment of the blown sand over settlements and farm lands. Thus very definite evidence has been established of sub-soil dating back to 6000-5000 B.C.

This consisted of a beach of sand and pebbles, which had been deposited over the beach for a very long period.

It would appear that the sand in the Feugré area of Cobo was deposited sometime in the 10th Century, because when the "Long House" was discovered it was covered with approximately eight feet of sand.

As far as Jersey is concerned Balleine records that on St Catherine's Day in A.D. 1495 there was a sandstorm which destroyed the fertility of the area known as Les Quennevais. Again in A.D. 1668 there is a record of land in the parish of St Brelade (which includes the Quennevais) being "swallowed up by sand and abandoned by its owners". In a paper printed by La Société Jersiaise it is also stated that their dune system is probably some 3,000 to 4,000 years old, so that the historical records can only be regarded as incidents covering a very long period during which sand continued to be blown up from the seashore.

Alderney too possesses large areas of blown sand, the best known of which is Longis Common where it has been reported that in places the sand cover extends to the amazing depth of eight metres. Longis is actually the place where many Bronze Age implements and a considerable quantity of Roman Pottery have been found.

There is thus much evidence of the destruction of fertile land by sand storms during historical and pre-historic times.

In addition I well remember when the people of Les Dunes at Vazon were complaining bitterly about the sand from Vazon Bay which was being blown into their houses and into their properties when storms blew in from the West. This was only stopped when surplus sand was removed from the area of beach involved. At first it was sold but it appears that it is now removed to other parts of the beach.

People passing along Grandes Rocques Coast road when a stormy westerly is blowing will appreciate the stinging affect of the mist of fine sand blowing in from that particular beach.

Clearing sand from the coast road.

Further afield there are also many places where ports have been closed, churches and other buildings buried and whole estates swallowed up by moving sand. The following places provide good examples of such catastrophies:—

North Uist in the Outer Hebrides, the Culbin Sands near Findhorn in north-east Scotland, Southport in Lancashire, the Parish of Parrahzabuloe in Cornwall and Margan on the eastern side of Cardigan Bay in Wales.

There is little doubt that apart from the very early pre-historic dune deposits it was the period between 1300 to 1700 that was the most important for the menace of blowing sand. During this period on the coast there is evidence of the increase in the frequency of cyclonic storms in the latitude of the British Isles and of a tendency for the sea level to fall thus enlarging the area exposed as beach giving increasing opportunities for the sand to dry and achieve a state in which it would be in a condition to be transported by the strong winds.

This lowering of sea level encouraging the blowing of sand from the beaches was connected with the increasing spread of the ice in the Arctic sea into the northern-most Atlantic and around Greenland where there were advances of the inland ice and of permanently frozen land.

Such phenomena were caused in the first place by a general lowering of temperature causing the locking up of much water as ice. Indeed the period with which we are particularly concerned has earned the title of Little Ice Age.

Although in this Little Ice Age there were definite fluctu-ations from year to year and from one short group of years to the next the surpluses of cold windy winter months were presumably due to North European countries blocking anti-cyclones.

There seems little doubt that we now have an explanation of the manner of deposition of our own sandy "Mielles" which became of little agricultural value to the Island when the area became covered with sand. However the early glass-house builders looking for cheap land built greenhouses on these sandy areas and were able to enjoy one of the sunniest areas in the Island, an area comparatively free from the fogs and mists which are so common over the district which includes the airport. No doubt they had difficulties in growing their tomatoes in their sand but most of them appeared to be capable of overcoming them.

At the present time most of the old greenhouses have been demolished and replaced by houses and two of the photo-graphs show Mr Ronald Machon and son following the instruc-tions of the authorities and removing the sand in order to reach the peat below it so as to build houses on solid material.

In all probability the peat represents an era when rainfall

Excavating sand at Albecq during the preparation for house building.

normally draining into the sea was completely blocked by large sand dunes produced in the same way as it did this year only at that time it flew landwards over the existing pebble barrier in large quantities and was not removed. Examples of the effect of the blowing of sand from the beach can be discovered by studying maps and observing names of districts such as "Les Grande Mielles", "Les Sablons" and "Les Dunes".

One photograph shows some of the peat excavated at this point in an area fairly close to the sea-shore but I possess a record of the fact that when greenhouses were built in the Vazon area it was possible to obtain loads of sand at a very cheap price, from the owners of the sand dunes of Albecq and Grandes Rocques. These were needed to raise the level of the land and to produce soil suitable for the methods used by tomato growers of the day.

Thus the building of the sea-wall had given a completely new future to the Vazon area largely freeing the area from blown sand. However now it appears that to build a house on a sound foundation it is necessary to remove all the sand in order to reach the firmer peat.

Now that houses are being built over practically all the

Vazon area it is pleasant to be able to write that these built on the site are indeed a credit to the builders.

One photograph shows the sand which had been blown up from the beach along the area still known as "Les Dunes" clearly indicating that sand has blown over the sea defences for an extremely long time.

Sand excavated at Albecq during preparation for house building.

La Mare de Carteret

LA MARE de Carteret, La Grande Mare, La Claire Mare, La Rousse Mare, La Mare à Vecheulx, La Mare Hailla and La Mare Revel were all lakes once to be found along the western coast of the island.

They were originally formed as a consequence of a considerable rise in sea level following a period of low sea level. But for the pebble barrier which the sea pushed inland, the low land along the coast would have been flooded by the sea.

But in addition, this pebble barrier had another function as it prevented the drainage water from the land flowing into the sea so that the ponds already mentioned were formed.

Thus La Mare de Carteret, like the Grande Mare, developed into a marsh with a pond which varied in size with the seasons.

Water-loving plants grew and flourished in the Mares and on their death they helped to form thick layers of peat which were separated by sandy layers.

Sand still blows over from the beach when conditions are favourable but at certain times in the history of the island the blowing sand has had a very great effect on the topography of the region and it is amazing how much sand was blown over Grandes Rocques and Cobo.

Actually the borings made at Mare de Carteret, which preceded the laying of a large drainage pipe through the area, disclosed a layer of peaty sand, one of peat and another of sand.

The presence of the pond is recorded in 1611 when the Mare de Carteret was owned by George Fascion, Seigneur of the Fief of Anneville and Le Conte, who on 6 May 1611 let to his cousin Macham for 13 years all the reeds and rushes which grew in his pond at Carteret.

He also gave his cousin the right to take eels and one draught yearly of carp — together with the use of such grounds as lay between the pond and the road which passed his house at Les Genats. The rent was to be 20 nobles of English money, five good congers, eight dozen of the best eels and one couple of capons. The Seigneur also retained the right to fish for carp and eels whenever he wished.

The level of the water in the lake fell substantially when a fair-sized drain was made to carry the water under the pebble barrier and into the sea. When the Mare de Carteret was owned by James, the fourth Lord de Saumarez, he constructed a canal by enlarging the existing ditches so that the children of his family and their friends could row down towards the sea.

A painting by the Hon. Marion Saumarez. The lady gazing at the canal was the Hon. Gladys Saumarez.

However, difficulties were encountered in keeping down the reeds and rushes so that they had to be cut back regularly, while care had to be taken to operate the sluice gates so as to prevent sea water from entering the Mare at high tides.

In addition the outlet, or 'noc', on the beach had to be kept free of obstructions which tended to be forced into the outlet in stormy weather. A blocked outlet would have meant the reappearance of the lake.

Eventually a footbridge was built leading to a little island in the middle of the canal and another spanned the water, enabling pedestrians to walk from one side of the property to the other.

A well-constructed path led from Saumarez Park through Home Farm and the dry, eastern end of the Mare de Carteret. This path must have been useful to Lord de Saumarez when he wished to communicate with his architect, Mr W. Quilter, who lived for a while in the house on the north-eastern end of the property.

When walking, Lord de Saumarez could, of course, use the bridge which he had constructed to span Carteret Road.

This route really formed a portion of the dream which Lord de Saumarez had conceived of creating a method of reaching his golf course, as well as the school which he had provided for his son and their friends in a building now known as Grandes Rocques Hotel.

After Lord de Saumarez's death, practically all his Guernsey property was sold to the States of Guernsey and they let much of it to farmers — this being the fate of La Mare de Carteret.

The late Mr Edward Falla held the lease for many years and it was later let to enthusiasts of the horse-riding fraternity, who worked hard to make the Mare de Carteret into a suitable field in which to ride and jump.

Bridge across road.

31

I remember the many occasions when I rode in the field, especially when we built jumps in order to practise our horses for a point-to-point race.

Much opposition was forthcoming from the riders and nature lovers when it was suggested that a secondary and primary school should be built at the eastern end of the field.

These objections were of no avail, although a small portion of the canal was retained in the eastern part in its natural state and serves as the home of ducks and masses of reeds and rushes.

The remainder of the property was drained and levelled, use being made of the large drainage pipe mentioned previously, which runs from west to east across the field.

The drainage water is pumped out from an outfall which stretches far out into the bay of Long Port.

As could be expected, much trouble resulted from the levelling of the land and the filling in of the canal. Extra drains were provided and much 'used peat' obtained from growers was used to fill in the hollows.

Eventually a beautiful firm green playing field was developed and in the meantime a fine school building was erected at the eastern end of the Mare to be followed later by tennis courts and a swimming pool.

Lord de Saumarez planted a great many trees around the property which now in their maturity are really beautiful. In addition, young trees have been planted in many parts including rows of alders which help to produce a delightful walk from the coast to the bridge over the Carteret Road at Les Genats, from which pedestrians can make their way to the interesting gorge and gardens laid out in what used to be scrubland to the west of Home Farm.

Anyone visiting this area can then walk out into La Ruette de la Tour and from there to Saumarez Park.

Farmers and Cattle

BY the sixteen hundreds farmers appear to have settled to a general routine which they retained with minor alterations until the early days of the present century. The size of the holding obviously affected the efficiency of the farm management.

One can discover much information concerning the farming practice of 1645 in an article written by Prof. E. B. Moullin in 1947.

The following are the most important items found in this article which records some of the items listed in preparation for a farm sale:—

A grind-stone with an iron axle.

An iron hammer, a hatchet, billhook, sickle and anvil.

A churn and a stone salt mortar.

A pair of pincer tongs and a carpenter's axe.

A ship's plank.

A fork with a long ash handle.

Two forks each with two prongs.

An iron for use with hemp and a comb and a knife for use with flax.

Three tools used for destroying teasels.

Hemp and flax designated for making cloth for children.

Five sieves and a rake with wooden pegs (probably used for hay-making).

Two ladders, a spinning wheel.

A bushel and a deneral of wheat.

A corn tub or barrel.

Twelve sacks of rye and fifty-two sacks of barley.

Five hundred sheaves of barley in the stack-yard.

Big coffin-like containers with flax tops.

A long cart — a hand cart and a box cart.

A yoke and appurtenances for use with oxen.

Plough wheels — iron axle and appurtenances.

Two steers — three black cows — three red cows — four heifers (one black).

Two suckling calves.

Three ewes and two wethers — four pigs (bristle beasts).

Two red oxen — two black horses — a black filly and a black colt.

What particularly impressed me when I compiled this list was the presence of at least four black animals in the small herd of cattle. This impressed me because early in life I had been told that one of the reasons why black animals had all but disappeared was because of the efforts being made to form an Island herd of first class animals.

From painting of black and white cows among those of normal colour.

In fact I remember how animals with black noses were not welcomed into a herd because the buyers from England and America just did not want them. It would appear that apart from the black noses, the black colour has been practically eliminated from the Island herd but whether this has improved the quality of the animals is not really known.

Apart from the differences in colour there is no doubt that the cows of today are generally bigger, stronger and better built than the cows of the past. They are taller, longer in body and have well attached udders held well off the ground. This is probably largely due to better attention to breeding and feeding in such a way that the animals have all the necessary food ingredients as well as essential minerals.

Another difference is evident when one studies the size of

the herd maintained on this large farm of 1645 and compares it with the number kept today on a similar farm in Guernsey. This may well be at least sixty five. In fact a farmer who is well known to me took control of a rather small farm which had housed but five or six cows in a small stable but by improving the buildings and purchasing machinery he was able to increase the herd, first to 9 then to 11 then 22. Then owing to farmers nearby giving up the keeping of cows my friend was able to buy their herds and rent or buy their fields. In consequence he was able to raise the number of cows in his herd to 65 which was ten times the number with which he had started.

Many farms have been lost to the Island because of the cancelling of the Law of Inheritance ("Le droit de Préciput") which gave the eldest son of the dead parent the right of claiming 14 to 22 perches which in practice included the family house. The eldest son was also at liberty to reclaim the land inside the ring fence; that is to say keep possession of all land to which he had access without crossing the public

Maple Leaf Cora's Connie, property of Mr H. F. Gaudion
2nd lactation 4,695 kgs milk and 5.85% butter fat + 3.70 protein — An excellent record.

35

road. However for that part which exceeded his own share he had to pay to co-heirs a price which depended on the valuation placed upon it by the Constables and Douzeniers of the parish.

Because of this law farm properties were kept in the same family for generations but nowadays all the members of the family share equally and this very often leads to the necessity of selling the property and the dispersing of the family herd. In addition the buyer of the property often proves to be a wealthy business man or in special circumstances a wealthy immigrant.

Another change involves the replacement of hand milking by the use of milking machines and the use of milking parlours. The milking of the whole Island is then passed on to the central dairy and then on to the milkmen who deliver the vast majority of the cartons of Guernsey milk, as well as the packets of butter also produced at the Dairy.

This represents a completely new development in the method of butter making when one considers the many different types of churns once used and the method by which it reached the public. Today all this is changed as all butter making is carried out at the Dairy.

Other changes have taken place which would give surprise to the old farmers. The first one concerns seaweed (vraic) the use of which by farmers has fallen to a very low level, so that at the present day farmers are not taking the opportunity of making use of the valuable minor elements and the nitrogen, phosphate and potash found in seaweed. It is also apparent that farmers are losing the opportunity of benefiting from the humus produced by the seaweed.

Still another change that has taken place involves the abandonment by most farmers of the pegging out of cattle as this has been largely replaced by the practice of keeping the cows loose in the fields surrounded by hedges and electric fences.

Lastly we now have the very much used system of artificial insemination which is credited with producing considerable improvements in the cattle. In Guernsey the first notable improvement was the irradication of a very serious disease which was producing infertility in our cattle.

At the present moment I am informed that semen from Guernsey bulls has been imported from the U.S.A. and

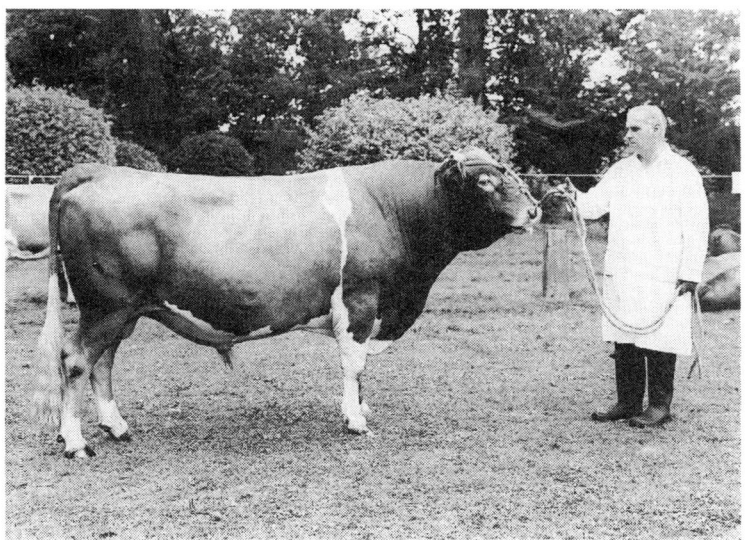

Pedro May Rose of La Masse — Champion at a Royal Show.

Canada. In fact it appears that the import of semen from Canada commenced in 1976 and that semen from a bull in the United States represents one of the latest imports.

The object of the use of this semen is to provide genes which have a strong effect on certain characteristics of the progeny such as stronger and better built animals, increased milk production etc.

The remarkable change in the way that cultivation is now carried out would also amaze the old farmers who worked with horses and simple cultivating implements such as ploughs, harrows, rollers, hand rakes etc. Instead of these they would be astonished at seeing the modern agricultural implements in daily use depending on diesel oil, whilst horses used for riding just look on.

Another tremendous change can be seen on the properties of our large farmers who now house their cows in purpose built structures which provide easy facilities for the animals to obtain shelter, food and water as well as providing arrangements to ensure the cleanliness of their buildings.

In addition very many farms are equipped with milking parlours where milking machines can be used to milk a

37

number of cows at the same time. In such cases it is usual for the daily milk production of each cow to be recorded, so that any weak producers can be identified and eliminated from the herd.

The feeding of cattle has also undergone great changes and gone are the days when every farmer relied on feeding with grass, hay, beetroots, kale, carrots, maize etc. Today simplification and efficiency have been introduced and the main foods are Silage, Hay, and Concentrates in winter, grass being fed only on limited occasions.

It would appear that better feeding and better breeding have produced yields of milk which are now very much greater than in the past and that this milk contains more butter fat and protein. In fact it has been discovered that Guernsey cows produce the highest amount of protein of all known breeds and of course proteins are necessary throughout life. They are said to promote growth and to be particularly necessary after serious illnesses etc, and as the body cannot store protein some should be consumed every day.

There is little doubt that if the old Guernsey farmers were able to return they would be completely shocked at seeing cattle of different colour and appearance to the animals of the Guernsey breed. To them this would have meant that the law of Guernsey concerning the preservation of the breed would have been broken.

However they could have calmed down when given the news that these strange animals would eventually all be used to provide meat for the public of Guernsey so that their presence is completely legal.

Poem in Guernsey French
Le Chant des Fontaines
La Chanson du Terrien

Dounai au roi ses biaux palais,
Sen biaux boucas, ses biaux parleux,
J'nen doun'rais pas chivraie d'panais,
J'nen doun'rais pas une douzaine d'oeux;
Mais j'aime du terrien la maison,
Couverte de tuile, couverte de glui,
Là, les mouissons font leux chanson,
Ch'est-la, q'nous'ot l'camas du douit.

Le citoyen aime bien la ville,
Le bien vêtu ses biaux habits,
L'savant a l'arts les pus utile,
I s'c'reit quâsi au paradis,
Mais la nature charme men coeur,
La tout est simple, tout est réel,
Les biaux courtis, les belles flieurs,
La tout est sain, et tout est bel.

Si mes jos sont d'couleur de bronze,
Et mes mains brûlaies du soleil,
La veritai est ma réponse,
Et l'hounete homme est men pareil;
J'sis patriote à tout bien faire,
En travaillant jamais gênaï,
Si jai quiq'fais un p'tit d'misère,
Personne ne peut me faire tremblai.

Honneur au terrien qui travaille,
Au vrai, au fort, au fier, au brave,
Sans li les arts n'vaudraient d'la paille,
Sans li, le comerce érai des entraves;
Honneur au terrien, maitre sis li,
Terjous content, et terjous sobre,
Ch'est chu que j'cré, et chu que j'di,
Terjous heureux, et terjous sobre.

Translation of Previous Poem
After T. Lenfestey
The Song of the Landsman

Give to the King his grand palaces
His beautiful possessions and his beautiful parlours,
I would not give a barrow-load of parsnips for them,
I would not give a dozen eggs for them,
Myself I love some land and the house,
Covered with tiles, covered with thatch,
There, the birds sing their songs,
It is there that we hear the noise of the stream.

The town dweller likes the Town very much,
The well-dressed his beautiful clothes,
The clever one has the most useful arts,
He thinks himself almost in paradise.
But it is nature which charms my heart,
There all is simple, all is real.
The beautiful fields, the beautiful flowers,
Where everything is wholesome, everything is beautiful.

If my cheeks are bronze in colour,
And my hands sun-burnt,
The truth is my response,
And the honest man is my equal;
I am a patriot at all doing well,
Whilst working never afraid,
If I occasionally have a little misfortune,
No one can make me tremble.

Honour to the labourer who works,
To the truthful, the strong, the cheerful, the brave,
Without him the arts would not be worth some straw,
Without him, business would have been impeded;
Honour to the labourer, master in his home,
Always content, and always sober,
It is what I believe, and what I say,
Always happy and always sober.

Le Moulin de Haut:
one of three mills used for
grinding corn

LE MOULIN de Haut or as it was once called, Le Moulin Susain, was formerly one of the three mills grinding corn in the area of the King's Mills (or more correctly, Les Grands Moulins).

This particular mill obtained its power from two mill streams now disused. One was an elevated stream running along the south side of Talbot Valley and the other, also elevated, was established along the side of the Fauxquets Valley, drawing its water from the Vauxbelets area.

Eventually the two streams fed the mill ponds at the rear of the mill itself and then carried on to help turn the mill wheels at Le Moulin du Milieu and at Le Grand Moulin du Roi which is now used as a pumping station under the control of the States Water Board.

Le Moulin de Haut had two mill ponds and two wheels fitted to the same mill. The upper one was the smaller and it operated the machinery in the upper part of the mill, while the lower one was responsible for the machinery in the lower floors.

Portions of the main shaft are still visible but the mill has not worked since about 1925, although most of the machinery is still intact.

I remember accompanying my grandfather to the mill in a pony cart in the early '20s and we brought oats to be crushed for use as animal feed. This was long past the days when flour was the chief product of the mill.

Le Moulin de Haut was owned for a considerable period by the Seigneur of Fief Le Conte and it is probable that it was rebuilt some time after 1356 following a number of French invasions.

These resulted in the wholesale destruction of most churches and prominent buildings, so that since this early date the

Le Moulin de Haut: wheels were fitted on a gable, and ponds were at the rear of the mill.

42

mill must have been restored a number of times to leave it in the excellent condition in which we find it at present.

Across the path is the present mill house which is a lovely building with an attractive front composed of carefully-cut granite blocks, the joints having rows of little black beach pebbles cemented between the blocks, thus producing a highly ornamental effect.

Other features of the property include the attractive climbers on the walls, a tourelle, 18th century panelling in the parlour, a sun-dial, the arms of the Lefebvres over the front door and a beautiful garden.

Mr John McCormack considers that this fine house was built in the years between 1550 and 1625 but refashioned in the 18th century.

He describes the ruined building west of the mill as a curious structure, as two stables occupied the floor of the building while a wooden staircase led to a kitchen or living-room above and was separated by a wall from a loft.

Another loft in the roof space was floored and probably used as sleeping quarters. It does seem possible that this building provided quarters for a valet.

Proceeding from these buildings upwards along the lane leading to St Saviour's, one is attracted by the gurgle of water entering a watering trough. From here the beautiful lane is just wide enough for one vehicle to pass, although here and there are 'rensages' which are places wide enough for two vehicles to pass one another.

Some years ago the floor of the lane was carpeted with grass. It represented the type of country road available before road-making, widening and repairing made necessary to cope with the demands of the day.

The damp hedgerows display a profusion of ferns, bluebells and other attractive wild plants. On one side the ground rises quite sharply towards the plateau of the higher parishes where we can admire a portion of one of the largest plantations of trees on the island.

On the side opposite the trees the land falls sharply down to a wet meadow which at one point has been made into a small, attractive lake surrounded by water-loving plants.

Old stories are told about the activities of certain residents who made use of the lane for smuggling purposes.

Arms of the LeFebvres over the front door at La Maison du Moulin de Haut. Note the pebble decoration between the granite blocks of the front of the house.

44

First of all the members of the group had to import their stocks from the Continent and when the smuggling vessel was ready to be loaded (probably in Vazon Bay) they are said to have used a method of frightening off sundry sightseers from their twilight activities. The same method was apparently used in other parts of the island.

It consisted of transforming the wagon into a hearse and deadening the sound of the wheels and of the horses hooves, by padding both with masses of straw. In addition, by means of special lights, the impression was given that all the mourners and others attendants in the spurious funerals were headless, and there is little doubt that superstitious persons seeing such a sight must have been very frightened.

Other forms of trickery were used to frighten anyone meeting the cavalcade and the word would soon be spread that a certain area was haunted so that people kept away from it.

Indeed, I heard recently of someone of great reliability and still living who had seen a headless rider in Le Moulin de Haut lane some considerable time ago. This illustrates how these fears can be carried on for generations.

Along the route people were warned to look the other way when the cavalcade passed by on its way to Vazon to load the boats waiting for them.

This made me think of Rudyard Kipling's poem in which he writes: *'Watch the wall, my darling, while the gentlemen go by.'* Of course such people were rewarded and there is no doubt that the whole community was either sympathetic towards or perhaps fearful of the smugglers, some of whom appear to have dealt severely with suspected informers. The law-breakers even bored holes in the Revenue Officer's boat so that the Governor had to advertise to try to discover the culprits.

It must be remembered that these escapades, which appear to have occurred in many places around our coasts, brought very much material wealth to the island. They also caused much displeasure to the controllers of revenue in England, who lost a very considerable sum from the taxes and duties avoided by the smugglers discharging contraband in coves and bays along the coasts of England — and even as far as Ireland.

Some of the beautiful trees on the Castel side of the valley.

46

Lihou Island

SPENDING a few hours on Lihou Island takes one right away from traffic noise and danger. Everything is peaceful especially in summer.

This little island stands well away from the west coast, separated from L'Erée by a channel which varies in width from a quarter to a third of a mile in breadth. Through this channel the sea bursts its way when high tide is approaching.

Visitors to Lihou must move smartly for seven hundred yards through the causeway to Lihou even though in certain sections they have to move over slippery rocks and pick their way between slippery pools.

Careful visitors can go to the isle and back in half an hour but if they wish to stay in the island for as long as possible they should aim at crossing as soon as the tide is first receding from the causeway so that they will have the longest possible time to spend in Lihou. However a watch should be kept on the returning tide and when it threatens to wash over the causeway it is time to 'get going'.

All visitors to Lihou should make enquiries about the tidal behaviour before they attempt the journey as on certain days in the month the causeway barely uncovers and visitors cannot make the journey.

As people approach Lihou they cannot help being impressed by the imposing residence of the owners of Lihou who are always helpful to visitors in trouble, I well remember what an impressive welcome I received from the previous owners (Col. and Mrs Wootton). I was particularly pleased with this welcome because on the way along the causeway the horse which I was riding had come to a dead stop whilst he surveyed the position obviously wondering how people could be walking about in what should have been rocks and sea.

When ceasing to admire the house and building, I feel that visitors will turn their attention to the ruins of the Priory which dates back at least to 1156 when it was established as the Church of Notre Dame de Lihou — this being confirmed on a Bull of Pope Adrian IV to the Abbey of Mont St

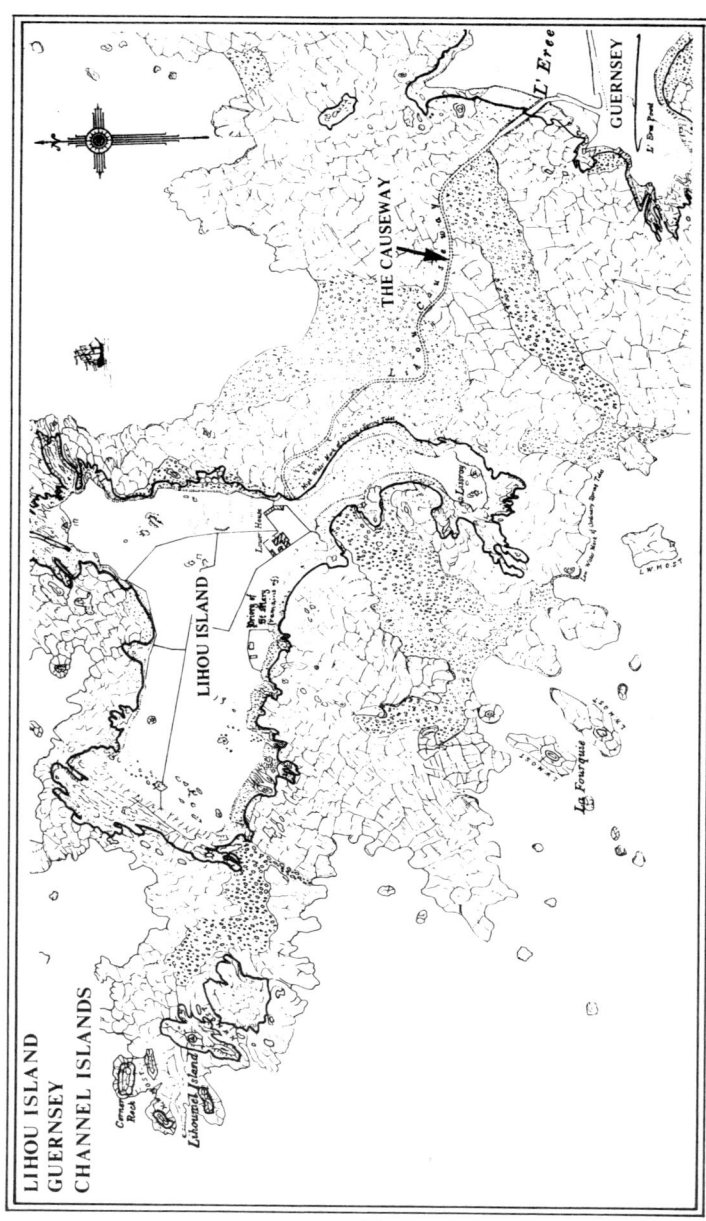

Map of Lihou Island.

Michel. This priory may well have been established as a challenge to the pagan worship which it appears was common in the neighbourhood.

Near to the position occupied by the Priory one finds the base of a tower or of a 'columbier' which could have been built on the same lines as the one owned by Mr Bob Froome at St Peter's. Such a 'columbier' was occupied by pigeons which provided food from their eggs and when killed provided fresh meat.

A little before 1304 Thomas Le Rover, a servant of the Prior, killed a monk of Lihou, called Brother John de L'Espin and he was killed in the Priory itself. A hue and cry was raised and the Bailiff came out with a force to arrest him.

Among his force was a Guernseyman called Ranulph Gautier who in the fighting which ensued, when Thomas Le Rover tried to defend himself, either by accident or design succeeded in killing Thomas so that two corpses lay in the Priory precincts crying for vengeance.

Ranulph Gautier fearing the worst, fled to the Church of St Sampson's and claimed the privilege of sanctuary from the Church authorities.

The Prior and monks, though proved to be innocent of any offence, took to their boats and sailed to Normandy and the Priory lapsed into the hands of the Crown.

It appears that soon after this Richard Paysant (whose name could well come down to us in the 'Paysants Estate') found that the Prior and monks had disappeared and had left two corpses lying unburied. Being so upset he failed to inform the Bailiff who reproved and fined him £15 tournois.

Eventually the Prior returned but was fined 100 sols tournois for having left the island when his presence was sorely needed.

Some years after his escape from the Island Ranulph Gautier returned bearing a letter of pardon from the King and he succeeded in getting back his goods and land.

He must have had some good friends to help him because he was twice made Bailiff of Guernsey and was a land owner in St Saviour's Parish in Jersey as well as in the Vale Parish in Guernsey.

However, he must have been unpopular with some persons in high positions because he was imprisoned in Castle Cornet and there put to death 'by many and divers tortures'. Those responsible for his death included Gautier de la Salle who was tried by the Bailiff and hanged in 1320.

In 1415 the Priory of Lihou which was of alien foundation was seized and brought into the control of the King, but in 1443 the responsibility was transferred by Henry VI to the Provost of Eton College.

In 1560 Thomas de Baugy of Mont St Michel resigned the benefice of the Priory of Lihou. This was probably the result of the Reformation and after this development the Priory and its services were allowed to fall into decay and to lapse entirely, although French fisher folk still lowered their mainsails in honour of 'Notre Dame au Peril de la Mer' as they passed the little island.

However it is very rewarding to read in the newspaper that a really sound and well organised 'dig' is being prepared. It is hoped that the results of the 'dig' will increase our knowledge concerning the buildings and the way in which the monks lived.

In 1734 an Order in Council decreed that the Island should be let on a fee-farm lease designed to grant long leases at a small annual cost to encourage the tenants to make the best of waste lands.

During 1759 the Governor of Guernsey ordered the demolition of the Priory Chapel to avoid risk of the French occupying the premises.

As time went by various persons took advantage of the grant of the Fee Farm Leases. Thus in 1815 Eleazar Le Marchant, the Lieut. Bailiff, obtained the Lease and tried to prevent local inhabitants from cutting and drying vraic (seaweed) on the Island. However, the Royal Court decided that the parishioners of St Peter's, St Andrew's and Forest were entitled to cut and dry vraic on Lihou.

In the 19th century Lihou Island became private property which made it possible for the Island to be taken over by people from outside Guernsey.

In 1922 a large whale was stranded on the Island and caused much interest in the neighbourhood, but eventually means were found to cut it up and bury it.

Eventually the Island was purchased by Mr Steven Duquemin and Mr Angelo Clarke and sublet to Mr Albert Best who farmed the land and started the extraction of iodine in his little factory using vraic which was gathered on the islet's shores. He was so successful that he supplied material ready for treatment to a plant in St Martin's in which it is highly possible that he had financial interests.

In conversation with Mr Dan Savident, an elderly man brought up in the neighbourhood near to Lihou, I learnt a great deal concerning the work involved in connection with iodine production. It appears that a box-cart and horse were used to gather the seaweed which was then dried on wire frames and when dry was burnt in an underground chamber.

At first it is reasonable to accept that Mr Best produced some iodine at Lihou but there seems little doubt that burnt seaweed was at one time carried in sacks across the causeway using a box-cart and horse and that the ashes were then picked up by a horse and van and taken to the iodine factory at St Martin's. The lane in which the factory was situated is still called 'Steam Mill Lane'.

In the late twenties this enterprise was killed by subsidised exports from South America, especially from Chile which had long held a monopoly.

During the war the Germans used the Island as an artillery target and shelled the attractive granite farmhouse. The heap of ruins remained undisturbed until ex-army Lt Colonel Patrick Wootton purchased the Island in 1961 and set about rebuilding the old farmhouse utilising the granite stone of the old building.

Colonel Wootton is best remembered for having established the Lihou Youth Fellowhip which he hoped would leave a lasting beneficial influence on those taking part. Every opportunity was given for worthwhile activities to be carried out and spiritual, scientific and sociological problems were discussed. At times singing occupied the evening and when it was possible barbecue meals were enjoyed on the beach. Each camp took place largely under canvas and recreational pursuits included swimming from a sandy beach or in the 'Venus Pool', sea fishing, boating, rock climbing etc.

A last look at Lihou can be of a considerable interest. Thus the low cliffs in places are seen to include a layer of smooth and rolled pebbles firmly cemented together into a compact mass forming a raised beach. The raised beach is an old shore line which shows that the sea once reached higher than it does now so that in other words Guernsey was a much smaller island.

Another interesting sight is on the fore-shore of the southern peninsula. There, on the fore-shore are two moderately deep holes in the rock hollowed out by the friction of stones washed round and round by the eddy of the strong tides. They are popularly known as the 'nuns' baths. Actually this name is incorrect since there is no reason to believe that there ever were any nuns at Lihou.

The Venus Pool is very popular and is situated in a chain of rocks running round the extreme western end of the Island overlooking Lihoumel and at high water it is completely submerged and washed clean by every tide so that it does not need chlorination or any similar treatment.

Venus Pool.

The Magic Well

A FEW years ago through the kindness of Miss L. P. Vessey I had the opportunity of re-visiting the area of her magnificent estate of St George which has considerable contact with past ages.

Here the Holy Well of St George can be seen which although somewhat modernised deals with the same water as it did in pre-historic days when it was regarded with awe by the pre-Christian population of the Island.

This awe is likely to have been engendered by a number of reasons such as the wonder aroused by the fact that the water gushed out of the ground and brought relief to humans suffering from skin and other complaints.

The result of course was that such a spring was given the credit of being a magic well. Such then the Well of St George attained its name and legends after the coming of the Christian religion to the Island.

Holy Well.

Thus the Well which continued to attract so many people was Christianised and a chapel was built near to it and recorded by Pope Adrain IV in 1155.

According to Metivier, a Guernsey writer of repute who lived at St George for many years, Dom Robert de Thorigne the Abbot of Mont St Michel visited the Island in 1156 and recorded that Guillaume Gatin the priest of the chapel had indicated his wish to resign and to enter a monastery. The reason for his resignation was recorded as being that he found the Castel to be far too gay and worldly. One wonders what he would say if he could return again to his duties.

Subsequently Dom Robert went to St George and appointed Godefrie Vivier to the vacant benefice. The induction appears to have been carried out by a representative of the Comte of Chester on whose "Fief" the chapel had been built. Eventually the chapel and the surrounding land became a sub-fief of the land of the Comte named La Fief de la Chapelle and all kinds of legends are recorded in connection with this property.

One such legend would have it that St George and St Patrick happened to meet upon this Island. St Patrick was most impressed with Guernsey and decided to make it his own but St George also laid claim to it. Avoiding a quarrel each decided to refrain from laying claim to Guernsey, but each to give it a blessing. Thereupon St Patrick declared that whilst trees stood and herbs grew no venomous insect, viper, snake or bloated toad should ever be found on Guernsey. St George in his turn smote the earth and a spring gushed out into a keep-pure fountain the waters of which St George maintained would heal many diseases and bless the owner of the area around it whose bread would never fail, nor his house become childless whilst the well was preserved untainted.

Another legend could have a certain content of truth in it. It is about the owner of the Estate who had an only son about six years of age who was thus the heir of the property. The boy was good looking, fearless and so well behaved that his mother loved him dearly.

Once, a friend of his fathers' returning from a long journey gave the boy a canary which he had brought from a distant land. The boy was delighted and kept the bird secure in a cage, but once whilst the boy was feeding his bird it escaped and the little boy chased it from tree to tree and bush to bush until he came to the well into which the bird entered. The little boy then leaned over the low front wall of the well and would most certainly have fallen into it and drowned had his attention not been drawn by the neighing of a horse behind him, and when he looked back, what should he see but the fiery head of St George's beautiful horse.

That moment saved the little boy and soon afterwards the bird flew out of the well and settled on the little boy's hand.

A painting was made of this incident and the boy, his canary bird, the well and the horse could be seen hanging in the owners house.

Superstition has also invested the area with further sightings of St George's famous fire-breathing charger careering around the lake.

A superstition maintains that if a maiden visited the well, fasting and in silence, on nine successive mornings, carefully depositing a piece of silver in the niche made for this purpose, she was assured of marriage within nine times nine weeks and by looking into the well with a keen wish to see the face of her future husband it would be mirrored in the water on the ninth day.

In the early days when the Roman Catholic beliefs were introduced into Guernsey because of the reported interest shown in St George, there is little doubt that the priest would have accepted the statement made by the girl concerning having seen the face of a man who was probably well known to both of them. Should he resist the idea of marriage with the girl involved the priest could well insist that this was a miraculous event and that the couple should be married straight away in the near-by chapel.

One cannot ignore the Cross in St George Estate which was erected in Christian times to help mark the Church path to Castel Church. Finally we must not forget the dolmens in the Estate which added to the atmosphere of the neighbourhood, although no one can explain how they originated.

Note: Dolmens no longer exist here.

Mysterious wrecking led to free drink!
Wreck of the *Briseis*

A VISIT to the museum arranged in the Cup and Saucer (correctly named Fort Grey) would disclose the large number of wrecks which have taken place along our western coast.

However, none is remembered so well by the older generation as the wreck of the *Briseis* which, after sinking, scattered barrels of wine and of strong liquor along the western coasts so that a great deal of excitement and drunken behaviour resulted.

The wreck is also remembered because the captain claimed that he just could not understand why the ship had struck a rock, because he had a great deal of experience of navigating our western shores and, in addition, he had piloted a French plane during the First World War which was stationed with others in St Peter Port.

It was on the first day of October 1937 that the large French ship, the *ss Briseis* of 3,000 tons which had been built

The wreck of the Briseis.

in Germany in 1914, was wrecked off the Houmet Peninsula at Albecq.

She was on a voyage from Oran to Rouen and carried a cargo of wine, spirits and phosphate.

The ship, when first sighted by a local fisherman, was seen to be sailing rather close to the offshore rocks, passing one danger point after another, until the fisherman felt certain that the ship could not help hitting the rocks known as the Grunes, the scene of many previous disasters.

After the crash the captain stopped all engines and then restarted them in order to pull the ship off the rock.

He then made all speed for the sandy shore of Vazon Bay, but his steering gear must have been damaged because the ship ended up in the vicinity of Houmet headland which is full of rocks.

Fortunately the rocks played no part in the drama as the ship sank before reaching them.

Soon, hundreds of people had gathered to watch the closing scenes, being attracted by the continuous noise of the ship's siren. As the ship approached the land it was evident that the bows were low in the water while the stern was rising in the air.

Suddenly the bows began to slide into the water.

At the same time the boilers burst and steam and water gushed some 30ft skywards.

The vessel sank completely out of view, leaving only the tip of the funnel and the masts out of the water.

I saw this disaster, and it left me with a permanent memory of the sinking of the *Briseis*.

However, trouble was to follow because the ship was carrying hundreds of barrels of wine and spirits from North Africa.

As soon as the barrels were released they were pounced upon by some of the watchers who, in their delight, regarded the appearance of the barrels as Manna from Heaven.

When the captain had realised the serious condition of his ship he had ordered the crew to take to the boats.

Having been given little time to collect their belongings, some appeared scantily dressed and carrying whatever they had been able to grab in addition to their lifebelts.

Mr James Le Page, of Lilyvale, Castel, was fishing within a quarter of a mile and he made for the scene of the disaster. He found that his boat was not powerful enough to tow the ship's boats. However, he invited the captain to come on board his boat.

Eventually the captain, who was extremely distressed, asked Mr Le Page to take him around his ship, after which the captain returned to the ship's boats to await the approach of more powerful boats able to tow them.

Mr Le Page was heard to report that the ship had sunk in 12 fathoms of water, and that there could only have been about six feet of water over the Grunes when the ship struck.

The motor vessels which eventually towed the ship's boats carrying 27 persons were owned by Mr J. Jehan, Mr E. Girard, Mr W. Bewey and Mr T. Carré. All made for Grand Havre.

Fishermen row around the remains of the Briseis, *hoping that more barrels of wine will bob to the surface.*

At Grand Havre an amusing incident took place when bystanders helped to pull on the rope being used to beach one of the boats — suddenly the rope broke and they all fell in an undignified heap.

However the crew were very well looked after, especially when they realised that they could converse with the country people, the majority of whom were French speaking.

They also must have felt grateful to Le Baron de la Coudenhove, the French Consul, who was present to help to attend to any problems which could arise.

But what of the other helpers, which included the crew of the lifeboat, the J. B. Proud-foot, skippered by Captain Hobbs, which had responded to a maroon sent up at 3 p.m., but arrived too late to be of assistance.

In the same way the GWR steamer approaching Guernsey was informed by wireless telegraphy of the situation and resulted in Captain Richardson putting on full speed for Cobo and Vazon, having ordered a boat to be lowered immediately they reached the wreck.

When they arrived, all they could see were the funnel and two masts, in addition to the boats being towed away containing the crew.

Eventually the captain of the *Briseis*, along with his officers, were taken to the tragic spot by Mr Charles Guille, of Cobo Garage.

The captain appeared to be extremely distressed when they found that there was a gaping hole under the bows as well as possible damage to the keel.

As soon as possible a notice was issued to the effect that all salvage had to be declared to the Supervisor, including any barrels found floating around in the sea.

Out of the 300 barrels it appears that only a small number were declared; some floated far from the Houmet, being picked up off St Martin's point, and by the *Joybell* on the way to Sark, while some were encountered by the GWR Mailboat.

But all this time the local lads were 'making hay while the sun shone', some barrels having been broached on the seashore among the rocks.

The wine was either consumed on the spot or was used to fill bottles and containers of every size and variety including, it was rumoured, some with an unmentionable private use.

The results of some of the drinking parties were those that could be expected, as some individuals were very drunk.

Indeed, it was reported that one man was found lying under a barrel, a stream of wine just pouring out of his mouth as no more could be swallowed. It was also reported that in some districts fighting broke out between inebriated men.

Some were very much wiser and collected the barrels and took them home to hide them for future consumpton for many years ahead.

I was offered *Briseis* wine during the Occupation and I remember that there were two kinds of wine, red and white, and that it was washed up in two sizes of barrels — the large one (ponchon) or hogshead, and the little barrel. The latter

Mr Ted Foster, pictured with the salvaged bell of the Briseis.

was easily handled, but the hogshead required extra skill and strength.

As the various hatches became detached more and more of the barrels appeared until eventually small and very strong ones appeared which were made of metal, which could have been steel.

These were found to contain a very strong alcohol and proved very attractive to the naughty boys of the village.

To be honest, the wine being of the cheap Algerian type required further time to ferment in suitable conditions.

In this state it is not surprising that it was judged as being short of entirely palatable.

To conclude I must mention the fact that in 1937 divers employed by a salvage firm rescued much valuable metal from the wreck although rumour had attached sinister objects to the venture.

Le Grand Havre — Le Braye du Valle, fishing boats, wrecks and a whale

SOME while ago I received a visit from Mr Basil H. Gaudion of Les Hoffets in the Rue Sauvage and in spite of the name of the road along which he lives, he proved to be most helpful to me in my search for information about life in former days.

His main message concerned the date and builder of the fishing boat called the Hilda which had at one time been owned by his father Mr Nicolas Gaudion and himself.

Mr Gaudion said that the boat had been built by Mr James De Garis of Les Vinaires, St Pierre du Bois and was approximately sixteen feet in length and six feet in width.

I mentioned that I understood that Mr De Garis was quite keen on building boats with narrow bows which meant that they could cut through the water and thus increase the speed. However Mr Gaudion mentioned that a broad boat could possibly carry more sail in rough weather.

Mr Basil Gaudion and his father in a boat built by Mr James De Garis some hundred years ago.

Continuing, my informant said that the *'Hilda'* was a splendid little boat which was 75 years old at the end of the Second World War and when eventually sold to Mr Hamel the *'Hilda'* was 77 years old, the sale taking place because the father and son partnership had decided to buy a larger boat.

Actually Mr Hamel was lucky to purchase a boat complete with a petrol engine which had been fitted to the Hilda to increase its speed but at the same time mast and gear had been kept in case of an emergency.

Basil H. Gaudion.

Another gentleman owning a De Garis boat still in good order wrote to me some time ago from his home in Alderney. His name was Mr Jimmy Gould and the name of his boat was *'L'Hirondelle'*. In his first letter he claimed that although the boat was very old he was using it for racing and was hoping to bring the boat over for the Rocquaine Regatta but he was unable to face the journey because of the rough weather.

When he wrote again he sent me a photograph of a modernised "Hirondelle" which appeared to be very smart.

Mr Gaudion then related how the 'Ravensdale', a steam coaster, went aground in Grand Havre in 1930 showing me a photograph of the incident.

The ship must have approached the land in a thick fog because Mr Gaudion mentioned that when eventually the ship's steam hooter was used it sounded as if it was situated in the garden of the house close to the hotel, which was without doubt full of people awaiting the end of the adventure.

Strange to relate, although the ship approached the land, Mr Gaudion's opinion was that more damage was done to the rocks than to the ship, which he stated was registered in Newcastle and run by Messrs O. Dorey & Sons Ltd.

The ship appeared to be buckled here and there but three or four days later Mr Walter Bewey piloted the ship under its own power out of the Grand Havre and it was acquired by the Guernsey Railway Co Ltd who owned it for a few years. It was typical of the type of steamer seen here 50 years ago.

The Captain of the next ship to make an unexpected entry into the wide mouth of the Grand Havre in thick fog, made his entry thinking that he was on his way to the port of Guernsey. This was a ship from Torquay called "*Emperor's*

Ravensdale.

Queen" carrying 460 passengers and according to Mr Gaudion the ship when first seen had already passed between two formidable rocks namely the Black Rock and the Quenon.

Mr Hedley Bewey and his son appeared to be the first to approach the ship that was getting close to certain disaster and at the period in question I had heard it said that a Mr Bewey in charge of a boat had called out to the Captain of the slow moving ship asking him where he thought that he was going, so that after a short debate the Captain realised the error that he had made in mistaking the entrance to Grand Havre to be the entrance to the Little Russel.

Having stopped his engines he then asked Mr Bewey if he could pilot him out to safety. To this Mr Bewey is supposed to have answered that there was no doubt that the Captain had been lucky in avoiding several dangerous rocks and it was going to be difficult to take him out to safety. Nevertheless he carried this out with the aid of his son and Mr Nicolas Gaudion and his son. Together they piloted the ship with its 460 passengers to an area of safety. Not being prepared to turn the ship around in this dangerous rock ridden bay they demanded the ship be reversed out of the Grand Havre, but it was their knowledge of the positions of the many rocks which saved the ship, the crew and passengers.

My visitor's next recollection was of the complete and sad loss of a fine steamer which occurred on the first day of February 1898. The ship was the 'Channel Queen' and was owned by the Channel Islands Steamship Company and was a twin screw steamer only three years old. It was on a passage from Plymouth to Guernsey under the command of Captain Collins and was carrying a considerable number of passengers.

Unfortunately, in fog and bad light, the ship hit La Rocque Noire (The Black Rock) which lies some distance from the entry into Grand Havre.

The incidents connected with the rescue of 40 passengers and crew members have certainly not been forgotten by the brave rescuers who are still alive today. In the interests of humanity and with their fishing boats they braved the rough sea to save life. A sea which had already overturned the steamer's boats because of the extreme turbulence around the Black Rock.

I was able to obtain the names of the four men who were

Channel Queen wrecked, not at Port Soif but outside.

prominent in their efforts to save life using their fishing boats. They were Mr Lennox Gaudion, Mr Albert Gaudion, Mr Nicolas Gaudion and Mr Bewey.

In spite of the efforts of these brave men twenty persons were drowned and buried in a grave to be seen on the east side of St Sampson's Church.

Mr Basil Gaudion's next reminiscence of an exciting scene in Grand Havre was of a lighter nature as it dealt with the fate of a complete stranger to the Island — a huge whale.

It appears that the whale was first seen by several fishermen who did all that they could to send it back to the open sea but to no avail. Eventually the whale was found lying on the rocks and the general opinion among on-lookers was that the whale had broken its neck.

However when the tide rose the whale was towed to a place higher up the beach where it lay for a week or so and attracted a large number of visitors. Finally it was cut into pieces and buried above high water mark below Hotel Houmet.

I was most interested when Mr Gaudion showed me a rib, taken from the whale, which was exactly four feet in length. He also showed me what he called a "tooth" which had been taken from the whale's mouth. Actually it was an unusual tooth because it had brown "whiskers" hanging down from it and Mr Gaudion told me that such "whiskers" hung from the teeth of whales in order to catch plankton which provide valuable food for the whales.

During Mr Gaudion's visit I was most interested to hear stories of events which had occurred in "Le Grand Havre" but in the first place they led me to wonder at all the changes which had taken place in this wide bay. At one time the waters of this bay penetrated inland to St Sampsons thus separating Le Clos du Valle from the remainder of the Island with the Church of St Michel, L'Ancresse and a very large area of land in comparative isolation.

What still puzzles researchers concerns the actual depth of water possible in the waterway, the type of craft able to pass through from the bay to St Sampson's, as well as the type of construction used to make the two causeways that permitted some communication between these two completely separated portions of the Island. With regard to transport it seems obvious that flat bottomed barges must have been used when the tide was suitable.

The two principle causeways were Le Pont St Michel which enabled worshippers to reach the Church and Le Pont Colliche which ran from the south side of the Braye to a point near La Bailloterie.

At St Sampson's a definite bridge existed under which the excess water drained into the harbour. Apart from the bridge

Whale ready to be buried in the sand.

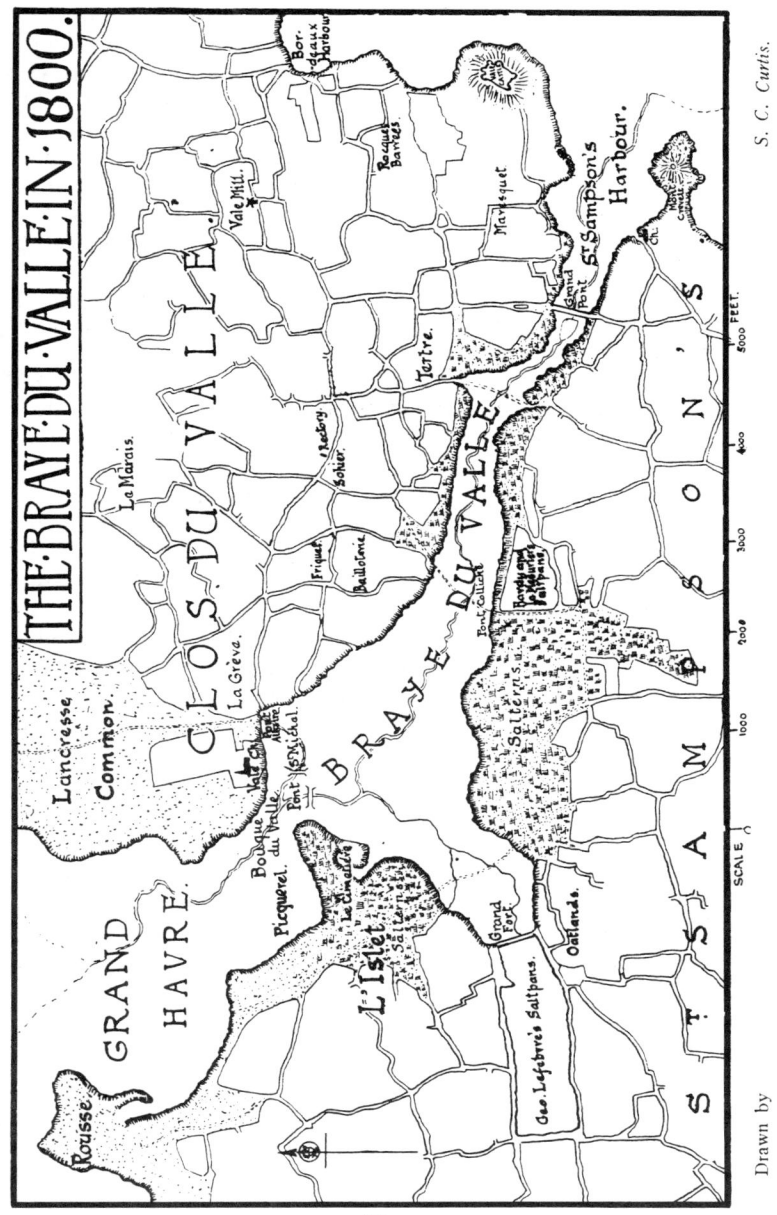

THE·BRAYE·DU·VALLE·IN·1800.

GRAND HAVRE.

Rousse

Lancresse Common.

CLOS·DU·VALLE.

La Marais.

La Grève.

Vale Mill.

Bor-deaux Harbour.

Racquet Barnes.

Maraquet.

St Sampson's Harbour.

St. SAMPSON'S

Friquet.

Baulorue.

Soluer.

Rockery.

Tortva.

Pont Colliet

Bouque Houillais
Picquerel. du Valle.

La maison

St Michal.

Bouque. du Valle.

L'Islet.

Grand Fort.

Geo. Lefebvre's Saltpans.

Oatlands.

BRAYE DU VALLE.

Saltpans.

ST. SAMPSON'S

SCALE 0   1000   2000   3000   4000   5000 FEET.

Drawn by   S. C. Curtis.

at St Sampson's a bridge existed which made it possible for individuals to cross the muddy waters below Lefebvre's Salt Pans. Strangely enough the remains of this bridge are now used by persons on foot to cross over the area which once was part of the Braye.

What is known is that at a time when an invasion from the French was highly possible the Commander-in-chief Lieut. Gen. Sir John Doyle the Lieut. Governor, being concerned at the vulnerability of the Clos du Valle and with the possibility that it could become a suitable point for an attack on the Island, decided to reclaim the Braye du Valle. This would have enabled troops and artillery to be rushed to L'Ancresse in the event of a French Landing.

In 1806 the British Government undertook the immense task of filling in the Braye, damming its extremities and obtaining filling material from sources quite unknown to the present generation.

The work was carried out quickly and the reclaimed area was sold for what was then probably considered to be a reasonable figure.

Along the southern shores of the Braye du Valle had been Salt Pans and Salterns. The proprietors were compensated for their loss and Guernsey's area was considerably increased. Eventually the area which had been influenced by the waters of the Braye was developed into an important area for housing, agriculture and horticulture.

The Privateering Era

IN THE course of Guernsey's development during the last few centuries there have been remarkable changes in the manner in which the Island has retained its prosperity.

Among these money making enterprises were the following: Knitting, mainly of 'Guernseys,' fishing, agriculture involving the sale of cattle to various parts of the world, the export of stone, and of horticultural produce, the practices of Smuggling and Privateering, shipbuilding and then at a later date Tourism, Industrial Undertakings, Banking, etc.

One of the industries which for a period of time was most successful financially was Privateering which involved the capturing of enemy ships of many sizes by means of Brigs – Brigantines – Cutters – Luggers. etc.

Those wishing to get involved in this work set out to adapt ships of many sizes so as to equip them for Privateering. To do this the chosen vessels were usually fitted with guns which were manned not only by sailors but with strong and able landsmen who were prepared to fight if the necessity arose.

The Channel Islands appear to have had a 'lion's share' of the prizes, a term which meant that the Guernsey vessels were able to capture very many vessels belonging to the countries with which England was at War and so benefit from the value of any prizes which they captured.

The fact that the privateers of the Islands were particularly successful is illustrated by the following which is a translation of a letter from the Governor of Cherbourg.

'These two islands (i.e. Guernsey and Jersey) are the despair of France at the breaking out of each war, through their remarkably active privateers, which always commence by capturing a great number of vessels and destroying all communications and commerce between the Channel ports, before France can adopt any precautionary measures to protect her coasting marine by vessels of war. The habit of encountering the dangers of the sea renders the natives very brave; they have well disciplined regiments of militia, excellent marksmen who alone are almost capable of replacing any enemy which might descend on their shores. Animated by a true sense of their own interest, their attachment to the English government is devotedly loyal.

'Good neighbours during peace, closely united by the contra-band trade, which enriches them, with the inhabitants of the neighbouring coasts of Normandy and Brittany they become formidable enemies when war is declared, or rather, they are always in a state of warfare, now against the custom-house officers of the two kingdoms, now against the French com-mercial marine. A population of this character greatly enhances the natural strength of these Islands.'

L'Invention. *French vessel of 489 tons built Bordeaux in 1801 as a privateer, and captured on her maiden voyage by the Royal Navy. Sold as a prize in 1801 and bought by Carteret, Priaulx & Co. of Guernsey. The four masted rig is unusual for the period and her size is more in keeping with an armed blockade runner than as a privateer. A fast turn of speed was to become useful when the islanders were tempted by the rewards of smuggling.*

The privateering activity started in earnest in 1692 when at the Battle of Cap de la Hague the French fleet was practically destroyed. It was at this action that John Tupper with his 'Mammouth Galley' destroyed four French ships as they tried to escape through the Race of Alderney.

There was a serious possibility that someone in a ship could be seriously wounded or even killed as the bigger ships of both sides tended to be quite heavily armed and were looked upon as additions to their countries' navies.

Much depended on the Captains' skill and audacity when over-hauling enemy vessels and if necessary boarding them. Captains also had to have the necessary skill and power in order to obtain the maximum efforts from their crews.

However the main objective of the Captain was to avoid a fight and the loss of men and yet to achieve the capitulation of the enemy. A great help to him was the fact that most of the enemy ships were trading vessels, especially in the war with France when the Channel Island privateers attacked and captured French vessels being used to carry goods from one French port to another.

It is even reported that one boat loaded with sufficient men to row in turns was able to capture a considerably stronger opponent. This meant that the small crew not only captured this boat but also the goods that were being carried.

Another curious case occurred when a vessel re-captured the 40-ton Guernsey sloop called the *Dispatch* and captained by William Le Lacheur. It had been captured by a French privateer while sailing from Southampton to Guernsey with a cargo of flour and with three women and sixteen soldiers as

Photograph of Letter of Marque. Note photograph of George III.

passengers. However all went well because she was re-captured near Cap de la Hague by a friendly ship.

As a result of the heavy responsibilities placed upon the Captain of a privateer, 'Letters of Marque' were issued to every Captain and written in such a way as to be suitable documents to enlighten the Captain of the special responsibilities likely to arise in connection with the ships of the country which he had declared himself ready to capture.

It would appear that a special 'Letter of Marque' was required for each country that the Privateer Captain and his financial supporters wished to attack. Thus I possess one 'Letter of Marque' referring to Spain and another referring to the American Colonies which had revolted against English rule and each of these 'Letters of Marque' was issued to Captain Dennis Le Pelley.

From 1793 to 1801 it appears that 235 'Letters of Marque' were issued to Guernsey Captains which then could act against France and its allies.

Again from 1803 to 1814, 602 'Letters of Marque' were issued to Captains of Guernsey vessels who were then free to act against such countries as Prussia, Denmark, Tuscany and U.S.A. as well as countries which were still considered enemies from the list of 1793 to 1801.

LETTER OF MARQUE

GEORGE THE THIRD by the Grace of God of Great Britain, France and Ireland KING Defender of the Faith. TO ALL PEOPLE to whom these presents shall come Greeting WHEREAS the Ambassador of the King of Spain has by order of his Court delivered to Lord Viscount of Weymouth a paper in which it is declared that his Catholic Majesty intends to have recourse to arms under the groundless pretence of obtaining reparation for injuries supposed to have been received. AND whereas the said Ambassador has received orders to retire from this Kingdom without taking leave WE therefore having determined to take such measures as are necessary for vindication of the honour of our Crown have by and with the advice of our Privy Council ordered that general reprisals be granted against the ship, goods, and subjects of the King of Spain so that as well as our fleet and ships as also all other ships and vessels that shall be comissionated by Letters of Marque or general reprisals or other-wise shall and may lawfully apprehend, seize and take the ships vessels and goods belonging to the King of Spain and the vassals and subjects of the King of Spain or any inhabiting within his countries, territories or dominions and bring the same to judgement in our High Court of Admiralty or in any of our Courts of Admiralty within our Dominions for proceedings and adjudication and condemnation to be thereupon had according to the course of Admiralty and the Laws of Nations AND WHEREAS we by our commission under our Great Seal of Great Britain bearing date the twenty-third day of June one thousand seven hundred and seventy-nine have willed required and authorized our commissioners for executing the office of Lord High Admiral of Great Britain or any person or persons by them impowered and appointed to issue forth and grant Letters of Marque and reprisals accordingly and with such powers and clauses to be therein inserted and in such manner as by our said commission more at large appeareth AND WHEREAS our said commissioners for executing the office of Lord High Admiral aforesaid have thought Dennis Le Pelley fittly qualified who hath equipped furnished and victualled a ship called Admiral Arbuthnot, of the burthen of about ONE HUNDRED TONS being square sterned, a plain head and three masts mounted with fourteen carriage guns carrying shot of four and three pounds weight and sixteen swivel guns and navigated with eighty crew of whom one third are Landmen and belonging to the Island of Guernsey, whereof the said DENNIS LE PELLEY is Commander and Edward Anley and sons and Samuel Lausa of Guernsey, Merchants are the owners and whereas the said Dennis Le Pelley — hath given sufficient bail with sureties to us in our said High Court of Admiralty according to the effect and form set down in our Instructions made the twenty-third day of June one thousand seven hundred and seventy-nine in the nineteenth year of our Reign a copy wherof is given to the said Dennis Le Pelley KNOW therefore that we do by these present issue forth and grant Letters of Marque and Reprisals to and do impower and authorize the said Dennis Le Pelley to set forth in a warlike manner the said ship called the Admiral Arbuthnot under his own command and there with by force of arms to apprehend seize and take ships, vessels and goods belonging to the King of Spain and the Vassals and subjects of the King of Spain or others inhabiting within his Countries, Territories or Dominions excepting only within the harbours and roads of Princes and States in amity with us and bring the same to such Port as shall be most convenient in order to have them legally adjudged in our said

High Court of Admiralty of England or before the Judges of such other Admiralty Court as shall be lawfully authorized within our Dominions which being finally condemned it shall and may be lawful to and for the said DENNIS LE PELLEY to sell and dispose of such ships vessels and goods so finally adjudged and condemned in such sort and manner as by the course of Admiralty hath been accustomed. PROVIDED always that the said DENNIS LE PELLEY keeps an exact journal of his proceedings and therein particularly take notice of all his proceedings and therein particularly take notice of all prizes which shall be taken by him, the nature of such prizes, the times and places of their being taken, and the values of them as near as he can judge, as also the station, motion and strength of the Spaniards as well as he or his mariners can discover by the best intelligence he can get and also of whatsoever else shall occur unto him or any of his Officers or mariners or be discovered or declared unto him or them or found out by examination or conference with any mariners or passengers of or in any of the ships or vessels taken by any other person or persons or by any other ways and means whatsoever touching or concerning the design of the Spaniards or any of their fleets, vessels or parties and of their harbours ports and places and of their intents therein and of what ships or vessels of the Spaniards bound out or home or to any other place as he or his Officers or mariners hear of and of what else material in these cases may arrive to his or their knowledge of all which he shall from time to time as he shall or may have opportunity transmit an account to our said Commissioners for executing the Office of Our High Admiral aforesaid or their Secretary and to keep a correspondence with them by all opportunities that shall present and further PROVIDED that nothing be done by the said DENNIS LE PELLEY or any of his Officers, mariners and company contrary to the true meaning of our aforesaid instructions but that the said instructions shall be by those and each and every one of them as far as they or any of them are therein concerned and observed.

AND WE PRAY AND DESIRE all Kings, Princes, Potentates and States of Republics being our friends and allies and all others to whom it shall appertain to give the said DENNIS LE PELLEY all aid, assistance and succour in their Ports, with his said ship, company and prizes without doing or suffering to be done, do him any wrong, trouble or hindrance, WE offering to do the like when we shall be by them thereunto desired and we will and require all our Officers whatsoever to give him succour and assistance as

74

occasion shall require. IN WITNESS WHEREOF we have caused the Great Seal of Our High Court of Admiralty of England to be hereunto affixed given at LONDON the ninth day of December in the Year of Our Lord one thousand seven hundred and seventy-nine and in the twentieth year of Our Reign.

Godf. LEE FARRANT   REGISTRAR.

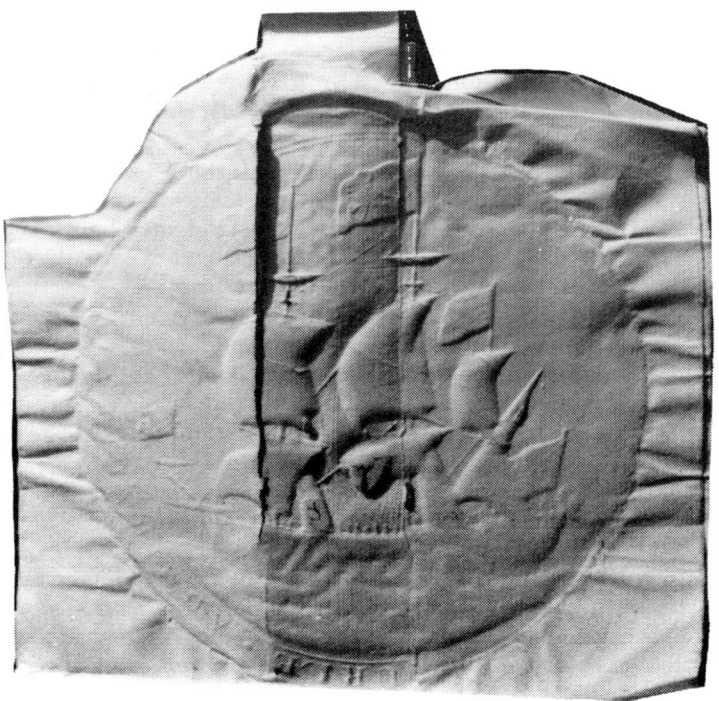

Seal at bottom of Letter of Marque. Great Seal of the High Court of Admiralty of England.

After reading the Letter of Marque granted to Dennis Le Pelley which authorised him to attack Spanish vessels it is obvious that this privateering carried out by Guernsey and indeed by all the Channel Islands was welcomed by the Government of Great Britain and of course it provided an opportunity for a great number of local people to benefit financially.

Thus it has been recorded that the Guernsey prizes at one time enriched the Island to the extent of a sum of money approaching one million pounds, an enormous sum in those days.

The profits which were made were certified by the Prize Commissioners whose duty was to discover the truth concerning the value of the goods found in a captured ship, details of ownership, bills of loading, etc. They also put questions to two or three witnesses one of whom would be the Captain of the captured prize.

All this information was sent to the judge of the High Court of Admiralty who would rest his decision to condemn or free the prize.

Business of the Channel Islanders with the Admiralty Court was facilitated by the presence in the City of London of a strong and influential community of Island merchants such as Peter Perchard and Paul Le Mesurier who eventually rose to be Lord Mayor of the City of London.

As a safeguard against Captains acting contrary to the terms of their commission each commander had to deposit a sum of money called a Bond. These bonds were generally entered in the sum of £1,500 and were generally entered into by the 'merchant princes' Paul and Benjamin Le Mesurier, William and Irving Brock and Samuel Dobree.

Further it appears that it was often the practice to deal with the profits in three sections so that when distributed one of these went to the Crown, one to the boat and crew and the third to the owners. In many cases the owners' section was divided into eight portions and the owners could take over as many of these portions as they wished and the profits were distributed according to the number of portions each owned.

These investors tended to purchase 'portions' in a number of boats in order not to lose everything because of one calamity. Many Guernsey men made fortunes whilst a few lost everything and had to be helped by close friends to try again.

However, it appears that from 1708 onwards the officers and men of privateers were allowed to keep the whole of the proceeds of their prizes. It is probable that the necessary services of the carpenters, coopers and labourers were also recognised as they had to be available when they were needed to work on shifting cargo from a prize to the privateer, to repair damage after a fight and if necessary to join in a severe combat.

When efforts were being made to capture two particular American prizes it was two Channel Island ships which were able to capture them, namely the *Clio* of 225 tons and the *Snipe* of 272. Having been captured the prizes were transferred into the *Two Brothers of Guernsey* and the *Mars of Jersey* and they were able themselves to capture further American prizes.

In concluding this account of the remarkable part played by Channel Island ships in the Privateering Era I feel that I should draw attention to the beautiful and well built houses and buildings around Guernsey which date back to the period when prosperity was brought to Guernsey by the Privateer Captains.

A Close Shave
(Adapted from old story)

NIGHT-TIME — a fishing boat containing five men, rolling idly on the choppy sea. 'What an uninteresting subject to write about,' you will say.

Uninteresting, yes if these men were trailing lines behind their boat but the mystery is that they were doing nothing of the sort, but simply peering into the starlit darkness. What then was their object in simply floating in this manner a quarter of a mile from Fort Houmet on the western coast of Guernsey? Actually their object was an unlawful and perilous one as they were waiting for a large French ketch, which would hand them certain goods including tobacco, brandy, wine and silk to be smuggled into England by English smugglers who would get them from these 'honest' fishermen and their friends.

All of a sudden a boat could be seen approaching in the dim distance and the figure of a man wildly gesticulating could be seen, could this be the ketch for which they had been waiting? Yes it was, far out of the darkness the form of a ketch gradually became visible. A subdued hail was given to the ketch, and immediately the sail was lowered and the anchor dropped.

With muffled oars the fishing boat pulled alongside, and after the usual hand shaking, the captain of the ketch, a jolly looking little man asked, 'Les douaniers sont ils occupes?' 'Oui, nous les a arrangis maite Henri,' came the answer from the fishing boat.

Pierre, the fisherman in charge of the boat who answered the query with regard to the coastguards was a broad chested, heavily bearded fisherman, 'Eh bien! ou sont ils mon ami Pierre?' asked the Frenchman following the reply given. 'Les douaniers qui etait a la Perelle ont yeue de dit que y'avait enne carquaison attendue par les bouanes gens du Grand Havre, et sont parti y vaie en si vite que possible.'

Translated the coastguards who were at Perelle have been

told that a load was expected by the good folk of Le Grand Havre and they have gone post haste to investigate.

At this the Frenchman seemed highly elated and hit big Pierre a wallop on the back nearly making that worthy lose his balance.

This conversation finished, the hatches of the ketch were uncovered and boxes, bales and barrels handed into the boat alongside.

The sea not being very rough, a big load could be taken and off went the boat for the land and ran close to a big rock standing just off the shore and here a dozen men seemed to have congregated, and quickly the boat was emptied and then returned for another load.

Let us leave Pierre and his companions and return to the land party and follow their movements led by a stout red faced man, named Jean Nicolle. They scrambled with little noise, unfalteringly in the darkness through a maze of rocks until they reached the grassy hollow where the necessary transport was waiting for them.

Unfortunately the coastguards returning from their wild goose chase to Grand Havre in their sailing boat heard a curious muttering in the darkness and sailed in that direction.

However when they were approaching the keen-eared Henri heard the wash of their boat in the water. This produced a scene of confusion and the fishermen were in their boat and the ketch was sailing away in an incredibly short time.

The fishermen headed for the little known cave known as Le Creux des Faies as they were in danger of being pursued by the Coastguard and his assistants. However with all the subtlety of Guernseymen the fishermen picked their way through the rocks in the darkness and purposely but carefully ran their boat among the rocks and then swam and scrambled ashore into a natural alley with cliffs on both sides which led to their refuge — the double cave of 'Creux des Faies'. In fact there were two separate caves in which they could hide, the small cave made the best refuge for small thin men who could disappear out of sight and a larger one penetrating far into the land catered for taller men. They were able to use this refuge because they knew that the tide was fairly low as at high tide this would have been impossible.

Eventually the smugglers emerged from the caves and made their way to the spot where their well hidden conveyance was waiting for them under the care of an efficient driver. Their next task was an important one because they had to help the smugglers to hide the goods in places in buildings on a number of properties. Carefully prepared 'dug-outs' under haystacks were used as well as cleverly conceived 'hides' in farm buildings.

The next day the coastguards were required to send a formal report to headquarters and in their report they described how they had chased a boat suspected of smuggling which had hit rocks and sunk. Finally they explained why no smugglers had been caught and the assumption was that they had drowned.

The Vazon Story Teller

AS far as one knows 'Story Tellers' ('diseux de Rislaie') have existed for a very long time and the tellers of tales in Guernsey-French were usually a joy to hear — that is if you had the time to spare to listen to them.

One day I met one of Castel's foremost story tellers walking up the road pushing his cycle before him. He greeted me in his usual cheerful manner addressing me as 'cousin' which was correct if one was prepared to delve in geneological records. He then said that he was sorry that he could not chat for a long time as he was in a great hurry but in spite of this statement he commenced his story carefully setting his bicycle at the side of the road.

My friend's name was Helier Le Noury and I always enjoyed his tales which to me appeared based on the truth. On this particular morning he was obviously keen on recounting the remarkable happenings which had occurred on a ship and in London.

Wandering about the deck of the ship Helier and his wife were struck with the spectacle presented by a lady traveller. Helier described her as a real lady looking like a princess and she filled him with admiration. Suddenly this 'real' lady came towards Helier and said: 'Surely you must be Helier — do you remember me?'

Helier was tongue tied that such a beautiful and elegant lady should bother to speak to him and above all to know his name but the lady continued to talk to Helier and said: 'Surely you must remember me as we both used to attend the little chapel of St Luke at Vazon.'

Helier still completely taken aback said: 'Surely you can't be Mary Le Grand who used to live at Albecq along the coast.' At this Mary said how pleased she was to meet Helier and invited him and his wife to visit her when in London. Finally, she gave Helier the number of her house in Park Lane.

When once settled in London the day came to make the momentous visit and having found Park Lane they located a

Helier Le Noury, once the well known 'Story Teller' of Vazon.

82

house with the correct number on the garden wall, but the house was not at all what Helier expected as the main drive was very long and led to a magnificent house. Helier then made a comparison of the length of the drive to the length of a large field in front of us.

This can't be the place said Helier to his wife — the house is much too grand and they decided to walk onwards trying to find a house with the correct number and style but without success, so they asked a policeman and he gave them very precise directions and would you believe, said Helier we finished up in front of the very house that we had previously examined.

'It must be here after all,' said Helier and they walked down the drive and all of a tremble they rang the bell. At this point Helier became very excited when he was describing the butler who came to the door wearing a uniform with silver buttons from his neck to the floor. He then described the hall which had a magnificent carpet in which their feet seemed to sink and beautiful pictures hanging on the walls. The enormous length of the hall was then described and finally the meeting with his hostess who of course was again beautifully dressed.

Her greeting over she then scolded Helier by saying: 'Well here you are Helier, I thought that you were lost, the food has been ready for ages.'

At this point Helier looked at his watch and repeated that he was in a hurry, not referring to the time lost in telling his story, but on leaving as a type of aside he said that he had found out that his great lady was really the caretaker of the magnificent house the owners of which were on an extended holiday.

Helier seemed to have a supercilious attitude as far as the German Forces were concerned. For instance although he had Germans living at one end of his house he was always ready to barter for wood stolen by the foreign labourers working for the German O.T. on the Fort Houmet peninsula. He once showed me a shed crammed full of wood.

Then as the need for fuel became most acute he opened up a pit on property that I am told really belonged to his son-in-law who had evacuated. Whether the property belonged to him or not, his pit was immediately opposite that worked by the States in the Grande Mare, but separated from it by a hedge.

Helier's pit appeared to be worked with efficiency which I felt was due to the experience which he had obtained during World War 1, when peat was used to augment the coal supply allowed for the greenhouses, but it was not until the end of the war that I learnt the real reason for this efficiency.

I knew that those working the pit for the States were dreadfully handicapped because the Germans would not allow them to use any mechanical means to empty the water out of the pits so that when they arrived in the mornings they had to use buckets and I assumed that Helier was working under the same difficulties — little did I know.

Needing fuel I ordered a two horse load of peat from Helier and I had the shock of my life when I had the bill which amounted to £1-10s. I went straight down to Helier's house and told him that I knew the enormous cost which it cost the States to dig their peat and I did not want a gift, but was prepared to pay the correct price.

At this, Helier told me that he was a business man and that he was making a fair profit out of the deal. Astonished I asked him how in the world he was able to make such a profit athough his price per ton was so low. His reply was that he would tell me when the War was over.

As soon as the war ended I tackled him on the mystery surrounding his peat-digging and he disclosed his method which involved the use of a syphon which he fixed to the water works pipe and that this was used regularly to keep the pit dry in spite of the fact that this would have been regarded as waste of water and against the law.

Of course such a syphon could be very efficient when properly installed and could suck water out of a pit but was really wasteful of water-works water.

Then I asked Helier how he managed to turn the syphon on at night after Curfew when it was against German orders for anyone to be outside their homes and especially dangerous where German guards were always on the prowl. Helier's answer to this was characteristic of his attitude to the Occupying Forces. He said: 'When we met the guards we had a chat with them and offered them cigarettes. Sometimes they only spoke French but that did not worry me.' He emphasised the fact that it was important not to show any concern and

84

certainly not to attempt to run away. Under such conditions he maintained that the Germans would never assume that they did not have the requisite passes, etc.

During a considerable period of the Occupation when the German forces confiscated all wireless receiving sets it was the custom of a small group of men to congregate at Albecq until on the approach of mid-day they dispersed to re-assemble at Helier's house to listen to the chimes of Big Ben and the news of the day thus keeping themselves abreast of the conduct of the War.

I was invited to join the group but instead I lectured them on the danger of the operation. I was particularly anxious for their safety because I had been told that the wireless set was on the table casually covered with a decorated cloth. Surely this was another example of Helier's contempt for the Germans and he was not caught chiefly because he gave no cause for his neighbours to report him to the German Headquarters and secondly the table of the living room would not have been the place where Germans would have suspected the presence of a radio. In addition the German soldiers living in the end of Helier's house did not interfere with civilians unless they were under orders.

Finally Helier met me one day and told me that he was in a dilemma as the Germans living in his house made a practice of calling on him every Friday evening to borrow his cork-screw but he said that so far he had refused to let them have so valuable an article. Instead he accompanied them with the precious tool and sat down with the Germans so that he could have his share of the bottle of brandy which they had obtained.

However the smooth run of affairs had received a set back as the Germans now wanted to buy the cork-screw, a suggestion which he immediately opposed as he certainly was not going to sell such a valuable tool whatever price he was offered by the Germans. Thus it appeared that the establised routine continued to take place every Friday night to the satisfaction of a least one of those taking part.

After the War I was asked by the Education Council to conduct and organise lectures for Farmers and Growers and on one occasion I had to meet a lecturer at the airport at quite a late hour. He had come from the Blackpool Region and I assumed that he would be tired after his journey but he indignantly denied this and said that he wanted to see how night steam sterilisation was carried out and that he also wanted to see some of the early sown tomato seedlings.

I thought that there would not be difficulties with either request and decided to call on Helier to see his seedlings. However, we found him in a contrary mood and lying back stretched out on his 'jonctier' or green bed. He started a sparring match in words with this Englishman, whose presence he did not appear to approve.

The visitor, obviously wishing to help this 'peasant', kept on talking about new ideas and new materials but Helier always had the answer that he had 'tried this and that' and did not really approve of them. Furthermore when the stranger mentioned Blackpool and Yorkshire, Helier said that quite truthfully he had seen the tomato growing in these regions because he had a son in each of these areas, who was responsible for running a tomato nursery. In addition he stated that he had visited them quite recently and had noted the working practices adopted.

We then went out with a lamp to see the tomato seedlings which certainly impressed the lecturer and from here we returned to the little extension at the back of Helier's house where he was still taking his leave on the green bed wearing his 'Guernsey' and reading the *Christian Herald* by the light of a pretty oil lamp.

Helier was thanked for his doubtful hospitality and complimented for his seedlings and then on leaving the visitor told him that as he had come to Guernsey to help growers there surely was a way in which he could help him.

At this Helier brightening up replied that there certainly was something which he could do and that was to recommend something that would make his 'old woman' work harder than she did.

This certainly caused a sensation as the wife concerned just appeared at one of the doors so that anticipating trouble, we quickly took our leave.

As we made for the car the lecturer stated that Helier was certainly not simple but actually appeared to be quite intelligent and in fact Helier was no fool and had actually been enjoying himself 'pulling the leg' of this unexpected English visitor.

He was remarkable in that he certainly was intelligent and worked hard to the end of his life. I sometimes wonder what he would say if he returned to see the very large area of Vazon greenhouses replaced by so many bungalows and houses.

Horsy Tales

TODAY the Island of Guernsey has a very large number of horses which are trained for riding in all its aspects. In fact there is little doubt that never before has the Island possessed so many equestrians of the calibre which we find today.

Long ago when I decided to ride my father's horses there was no one to teach me but I was determined to teach myself largely by observing others.

I was in my early teens at the time when I took the matter seriously and suffered my first fall when the mare I was riding at a gallop turned sharply to the right instead of turning left towards the stables. This fall caused some damage to my ribs but thankfully the pain did not last for a long time.

In experiencing my second fall the mare was more considerate as we galloped down the field in which steam sterilising was being carried out and she took the opportunity to throw me head first into the freshly steamed sterilised heap of soil. When I had rid my face and head of soil, I found that though dirty I was unhurt.

After this the mare and I were on better terms and I used to go for deep water swims at Vazon Bay. As I was sitting on her back I was lucky that she did not decide to swim on her side. However my father found out about this swimming and told me to stop because of the danger.

Soon after this my father bought a fairly light horse which could serve the two required purposes of farm work and riding and I rode him to a well known stable for advice concerning my riding.

I was expected and when I arrived at the stables I found that although it was Sunday morning all the drivers were there waiting and afterwards I learnt that they were present to see the fun.

When I arrived the owner sent one of his men to fetch a particular horse saying that mine was rather heavy for me. The man sent on this errand appeared to be hesitant but he went to a stable and brought out the animal which was all ready for a rider.

I managed to get into the saddle without too much difficulty but then the trouble started and the creature did everything in his power to throw me off and yet did not move forward more than a yard or two. Eventually I got tired of these antics and gave the horse a sharp blow with my whip and that set him off at a very fast speed round and round the field.

Daughter on pony.

According to what one of the drivers told me in confidence afterwards I was expected to fall off this animal causing amusement to the observers.

Finally the owner gave me his own horse to ride whilst together we went for a ride and afterwards I rode the owners horse at a Parish show. After this I felt that I had passed my certificate of riding ability.

It was about this time that my uncle's old horse died. He was a heavily built horse and it would appear that my uncle had been determined to replace him with a light and lively horse. However he made the sad mistake of attaching the horse to a peg in a field without realising the possible consequences especially as a heavy chain was attached to the end of the rope. This was meant to keep the rope down on the ground out of the way of the horse's legs but this did not work with this lively horse who took fright and galloped off dragging the chain behind him.

He was reported to have been seen jumping the sea wall at L'Etrainfer at Cobo and landing on the accumulation of pebbles which existed at that time and then it appears that he jumped back on to the road and set off along the coast as far as L'Ancresse where he was caught in a dreadful state still dragging the chain behind him.

From then onwards neither my uncle or his man dared to take him out of the stable and one day my uncle phoned and asked me if I would try to ride the horse. I agreed but on condition that my father came and helped me to put the saddle on and get the horse out of the stable.

Actually my father was remarkable in his ability to deal very kindly but firmly and efficiently with the average horse, however this horse was far from being an average one but my father and I were able with great difficulty to put the saddle and bridle on him. The next stage involved taking the horse out of the stable and getting the rider firmly in place.

At that point I told my father that I would stand on the rather high pig-sty wall and jump on the horse's back as he led him down the yard. The jump was entirely successful but this set the horse off at a roaring speed before I had found the stirrups but away we went and I made for Vazon beach, where he calmed down after a while.

Eventually another horse appeared on the beach which had entered for a mile race at the North Show then held at

Grandes Rocques. The rider asked me to gallop with him and away we went when suddenly one of my stirrups disappeared and I found myself hanging over on one side of the horse holding on the saddle by the tip of my right knee.

I knew that I was going to fall but I realised that the horse would bolt if this happened, so I drew my left hand forward until I was able to grasp the ring of the bit and let myself fall off this galloping horse.

P.J.G. on horse.

The shock of my weight on his bridle caused his hind quarters to swing around but still having hold of the bridle prevented me from falling flat on the ground so that eventually I remounted the horse and rode him back to his owner.

However there was no alternative. My uncle had to sell his beautiful young horse and subsequently I was sad to think of his death in the hands of his new owner when he bolted and was going so fast that he could not make a necessary turning and hit his head against a wall. The real cause of death really dated back to the mistake in tethering.

One incident that occured some years after which from my

point of view will never be forgotten concerned my daughter as well as myself.

We were cantering our animals across the dune which lies between the road leading to La Rocquette at Vazon and the road leading to La Rue des Goddards when the very nasty accident happened.

The first sign of impending trouble appeared when I happened to cross safely over a pool of mud. Knowing that my daughter was riding behind me on her pony I turned around to warn her of the mud pool but this completely upset the situation as my horse catapulted me into another pool of mud whilst he turned a complete summersault and landed in the road on his back with his legs in the air.

As I recovered quickly and immediately thought of the horse who was still lying in the road in an immobile condition, I rushed to him and to my relief he shook himself and got up and to my great relief was unhurt.

However what struck me as unexplainable were the bursts of laughter from the dune which I found came from my daughter on her pony. I could not understand the laughter until I realised that both horse and rider were covered in mud from head to toe.

The next thing to do was for me to get on the horse and ride back home and when we arrived my wife was awaiting us on the door step. When she saw the condition of horse and rider she too burst into laughter quite forgetting that we might have been hurt.

However after a bath for the rider and a thorough wash for the horse everything was back to normal except that I pretended to be rather annoyed with the attitudes of those from whom some sympathy could have been expected.

Ma Tànte

Ma tànte est une mênagère
Comme je cré qu'é qn'y-en a pouit,
Ou síl en est, g'ny en a guere
Dítaile en tout Guernesi:
M'n onclle a biau ill dire: "Ma Chère,
Reste acouare ùn p'tit su l'dun"
A quatre heures all est dans làire –
Hiver, étai, ch'èst tout ùn.

"Allon," s't-alle "hors de la pllume,
Rascaille de baisses et valets!"
Ah dame! a vous les arrûme.
Et leux apprend l'heure qu'il est.
Car, amains bien qu'a seit dame,
A travaille à fileur de corps,
Coum'si ch'tait la pus paûre femme,
Par dedans et par dehors.

Les jours de lavin man finge,
A prend so pllèche au baillot,
Etend quâsi tout sen linge,
Et, si l'faut, joue du ribot,
Bouit les cauches, empèse et ferre
Moucheux coueffes et tout chunna,
Et jusqu'à la gnièt toute nère,
Terjoûs mine et terjoûs va.

Pour en v'nir à la bouane femme,
(L'Bouan Gu m'pardoune de menti)
Il est seur qu'a n'a dans l'âme
Ni chéritai, ni piti:
Qu'une paûre queriature Ilê d'mànde
Une vieille craûte au nom de Gyu,
A llî dit "Va – t-en caîmànde!
L'abîme, la câche et cllôt l'u.

93

All a des haînes coum' le guiable,
L'avarice au vier Judas,
Des caûdrioles indomptables,
Une làngue de vipère hélas!
S'elle, ou les femmes de sa sorte,
Gagnent à l'us de Paradis,
Che s'ra mais que j'les y'porte,
Et la s'maïné ès quat' Jeudis!

Taken from Poetry written by George Métivier.

My Aunt

My aunt is a housekeeper,
As I believe there are not any such,
Or if there are, they are but few,
Similar in all Guernsey:
My uncle in spite of telling her: "My dear,"
Stay a little longer on the downy bed,"
At four o'clock she is on the floor –
Winter, summer, it's all the same.

"Come on," says she, "out of the feathers
Rascals of maids and men servants!"
Well darn it all! she puts them to rights,
And draws their attention to the hour;
Though realising well that she is a lady,
She works with all her strength of her body.
As if she was the poorest of women,
Working inside and outside.

The washing days believe me,
She takes her place at the tub,
Spread out practically all the clothes,
And if it is necessary uses the "ribot",
Boils the stockings, starches and irons
Handkerchiefs, and all that,
And until the evening is quite dark,
Always the same and on the go.

94

To return to the good lady,
(May the good God pardon me for lying)
It is certain that she has not in her soul
Any charity or any pity:
When a poor creature asks her
For an old crust in the name of God,
She tells her: "Get out beggar!"
Insults, drives her away and closes the door.

She has the malice of the devil,
The avarice of the old Judas,
Fits of unmanageable rage,
A viper's tongue alas!
If she or woman of her kind,
Reach the door of Paradise
It will be when I carry them,
And in the week of four Thursdays!

For Pions a kiss for every girl they met

THE organisers of the reenactment of the Chevauchée de St. Michel at the time of the 1987 Guernsey Festival are to be congratulated. They gave pleasure to a considerable number of people, especially at Sausmarez Manor.

The questions which readers have been asking me relate to the true role of the pions and the 'Table des Pions' (Fairy Ring) at Pleinmont.

La Table des Pions comprises one of the very few existing remains of the cavalcade known as the Chevauchée and can be seen at Pleinmont Point.

It looks like a beautiful round table cut out of a grassy slope and here countless generations of hungry horse holders or Pions have been refreshed after having trudged for many miles around the island from the site of the ancient Priory of St. Michel in the Vale, through St Sampson's, St Peter Port, St Martin's, the Forest, St Peter's and Torteval.

The serious duties of the Pions really consisted in being at hand, and ready to hold and help to control the horses

La Table des Pions.

P. J. G. at Chevauchée.

ridden by officials of the Chevauchée, which included members
of the Fief Courts of St Michel of the Vale.

However, the Pions had other duties to perform; being
chosen for their good looks they were given the privilege of
kissing every woman they met, whether gentle or simple,
married or single, governor's wife or labourer's daughter but
not more than one Pion was allowed to kiss the same lady,
so that she had not to run the gauntlet of the gang!

Having ridden in the staged Chevauchée of 1966 I can
vouch for the enthusiasm which the Pions exerted, especially
when they kissed two elderly gentlewomen strolling down
the Grange. These dear women obviously were astonished —
and showed it!

It was an advantage as an observer to be perched on a
horse and when we passed one house accommodating dancers
from a nearby hotel, the Pions did not hesitate. In through

the door they went, creating much noise, but everything appeared to be accepted in good fun.

My own participation in the Chevauchée was of a more mundane character as I was chosen to be one of the considerable number of riders allocated to follow the fictitious Governor, as a member of his escort.

We were all dressed in military-style, old red uniforms and

Pion c. 1768.

tall shakos. Actually it was the shako which caused all my trouble.

The evening before the event I dressed in my uniform and wore my shako, never dreaming that my horse, tethered in a nearby field, would object to my outfit. But he took one look at me and galloped away, it appeared, straight for the next parish.

Eventually he was caught and during the evening I visited the stable frequently wearing my shako. At first he tried to climb the walls but eventually he calmed down and I thought that my troubles were over.

The next morning I groomed the horse, saddled him, bridled him and tied him to an appropriate ring in the yard. I then went to get my shako.

When I emerged the horse gave one terrified look and tore away from his attachment and made up the road.

Sadly I followed and eventually met a kind farmer walking down the road with the horse. Having replaced the broken harness I managed to get on his back and we set off for La Hougue à la Perre (or Tram Sheds) but all the way I kept wondering what was going to happen when Rusty met all the other riders wearing shakos.

Fortunately, and to my surprise, he did not turn a hair and behaved beautifully all the remainder of the time. Such is the perversity of animals.

The task of the Chevauchée is usually accepted as being to keep the King's highway clear of all obstacles but the late Edith Carey and others have written papers which indicate that this was a role superimposed on other and much older duties. This can best be shown by asking a number of questions.

Why did the organisers always try to keep to the same route?

Why did the Pions dress in a most unusual costume?

In 1768 they wore black caps (calottes) each with a red ribbon at the back, a ruffled shirt (une chemise à manchette), with black ribbon wrist-bands and a black ribbon round the neck, white breeches with ribbons tied round the knee, white stockings and red ribbons on their wands.

Why did the musicians wear long white smocks?

Why did the cavalcade stop at certain spots and indulge in dancing and singing?

Why was a cavalcade organised by the Fief St Michel of the Vale allowed to traverse the island roads crossing through other fiefs giving instructions and making demands concerning the state of the roads?

What can be the explanation for the practice of rolling a stone into a house as soon as the cavalcade approached and why did the Chevauchée circle around certain other stones?

Members of Chevauchée at La Table des Pions.

Why were the Pions allowed to kiss all the women whom they met?

Finally, why was the miller of the King's Mills required to produced a sample of freshly-ground wheat flour?

To expect anyone to explain all these queries is pointless but a general explanation is that the Chevauchée has been built up over three vastly different eras.

First came the period of pre-history of which we really know very little, especially concerning the religious practices which evolved over an extremely long time. But there is little doubt that many of the questions could be answered if we knew more about this period.

Indeed it has been suggested that the organisation of the

route and even the kissing may well have been aimed at influencing the fertility of the cultivated land and possibly of the inhabitants of the island.

Although no record exists of the dances performed and of the songs the people sang when swirling around a central object there seems no doubt that this object would have been a primeval altar, a symbolic deity or indeed a preparation for a human sacrifice to be carried out at the conclusion of the dance.

With the coming of Christianity it would appear that the missionary priests were loath to risk destroying all remnants of pre-Christian religious practices and instead Christianised them by erecting crosses near them, or even building churches in their vicinity.

Thus they Christianised the Chevauchée, eventually putting it under the control of the Feudal Court of St Michel.

No doubt priests took part in the Chevauchée and drew the attention of all present to the existence of the crosses.

It is also likely that they continued to regard the cavalcade as giving an opportunity to bless the crops, grain and flour as carried out traditionally at the King's Mills.

The third stage in the evolution of the Chevauchée was reached with the Reformation, when almost all crosses were destroyed and the Roman Catholic priests had to escape to France. The Chevauchée, when eventually re-organised, appears to have transferred most of the care to civil authorities and the emphasis was then given to keeping the King's Highway clear of all obstacles.

Strangely enough remnants of the old, even pre-Christian, customs were allowed to creep into the ceremonials in spite of the fact that by this time the people of Guernsey had ceased to recognise any special significance in their dancing and singing, or in their curious performances en route. In fact they were out to enjoy themselves.

More reminiscences concerning
Mr Raymond Falla O.B.E.

A COURAGEOUS leader, Mr Raymond Ogier Falla, O.B.E., was a shrewd businessman as well as an astute politician during an active life. He came to the assistance of the Island at a time in its history when a man of his stature was particularly needed and afterwards was a great factor in helping islanders to overcome the immediate difficulties caused by the Occupation and to rise again towards an era of normal prosperity and happiness.

Yet in spite of all this he remains what he always has been — a true Guernseyman speaking the ancient language of his forefathers and possessing the true inborn humour so characteristic of the islander.

In spite of advancing years Mr Falla has a marvellous memory, a clear brain, and still views life as a challenge associating himself with many important aspects of his island home.

He has walked with princes but he has never lost the common touch and the island may never see his like again.

In an interview former Conseiller Raymond Falla expressed his views on the most important events which had occurred since he first became interested in horticulture.

He stated that the lowest level of income obtained from horticulture was in 1926 because competition from Holland on the English markets was particularly severe, as Dutch growers flooded the English markets with tomatoes from cold houses. Unfortunately Jersey was also producing tomatoes in late August from 2,000 vergees or more planted out of doors.

Thus Guernsey tomatoes paid up to the end of June but the remunerative production ended in July, the growers having produced an average of 5 to 6 lbs a plant. With the prices exceedingly low in 1930, Mr Falla and Mr Percy Dorey, endeavoured to persuade the British Government to put a tariff on Dutch tomatoes and flowers.

Raymond Ogier Falla, O.B.E.

At that time Dutch bulbs flooded the Island early in the year and they sold for a high price but later on cheap bulbs were available and buyers were the only people to make money from the flowers.

Eventually the tariff on Dutch fruit and bulbs was established and Guernsey benefited substantially.

Mr Falla was an observer in the early thirties on the National Farmers Union and helped to bring about the tariff.

In 1932 Mr Falla was invited to join the firm of Lowe and Shawyer eventually becoming a Director. He grew large quantities of bulbs for Lowe and Shawyer as bulbs forced in England benefited by being reconditioned in Guernsey soil.

Things began to improve as 20,000 vergees of tomatoes were grown outdoors in Guernsey, 10,000 plants being grown by Mr Falla's father and with this increased profitability growers improved greenhouse structures and methods of culture. Mr Falla also co-operated with the administrators of the Dutch Horticultural Advisory Service and this made him determined to establish a Guernsey Advisory Service to assist Guernsey horticulturalists.

A difference of opinion among the growers caused delay as some favoured the establishment of a Liaison Officer whilst others favoured setting up a small Experimental Station on the Island, but it was several years before a station was established in Guernsey.

In 1938 the States were informed that war could be imminent so that Guernsey exports should be rationalised.

Mr Falla was then made Secretary of the Emergency Purposes Agricultural Committee of 1938 and the Ministry sent representatives to meet the Emergency Powers Committee. As a result, early Potatoes and Tomatoes were sent only to named ports.

The deliberations carried out by the British Growers Publicity Committee of which Mr Falla was a member prior to 1938 formed the basis of the Tomato Shipping Law. This ensured after the war that shipping through local "agents" had to be abandoned.

The Occupation brought a general collapse of all arrangements but in 1945 shipping was organised in an orderly way and people could only ship to certain destinations.

At the point when the Island was occupied it was realised that ruling by means of a States Assembly was impossible and the Controlling Committee was formed and given plenary powers, Mr Falla being appointed to look after the Agricultural Industry. He later found himself also responsible for the Glasshouse Utilisation Board.

The growers found themselves, faced with the catastrophe of Occupation, with hundreds of acres of tomatoes left hanging on the wires producing absolute devastation. The recently formed Controlling Committee decided that the States would run the glasshouse industry by employing the glasshouse owners and their workers to prepare the greenhouses for growing crops of potatoes and vegetables for local consumption.

It was then discovered that the supply of seeds in the Island was at a low state and that the Island would soon run short of sugar, flour, meat and other comestibles and necessities.

The occupying forces were afraid of the situation and it was agreed that a Trading Commission should be established in France and Mr Falla was asked to go there to establish it. Before leaving the Island Mr Falla left specific instructions with those responsible to look after the various departments under his charge.

These gentlemen were all asked to appoint "organisers" to oversee the various departments. At this point contact was made with Jersey which joined in establishing the Trading Commission, and on the 14th August, 1940, Mr Falla and Mr Wilfred Hubert together with Mr John Joualt from Jersey set up their headquarters in France.

Mr Falla carried £7,000 worth of Occupation Marks and the gentlemen from Jersey had £13,000 worth of the same coinage. This was the commencement of the Purchasing Commission.

The Purchasing Commission lasted four years and very mixed cargoes were sent to Guernsey and Jersey including machinery for farmers, seeds for glasshouses, flour, sugar and, in summer, live animals were sent over and put out to graze. At times it was possible to purchase clothes, shoes and wooden soled foot-wear, but on one trip charcoal burners were sent over with a French engineer to install them.

In France when Mr Falla set out on a purchasing trip his vehicle was always driven by a German Chauffeur but a great many of his successes were due to his remarkable ability to speak a number of languages. Mr Falla was always well respected by the Germans with whom he was concerned; they even called him Herr Minister.

Mr Falla returned to Guernsey occasionally to be faced with the task of solving problems that had arisen in horti-culture and on these journeys across the Channel, Mr Falla remembers that there was less danger from the Navy than from the planes which flew above the German ships which they had to use.

Two or three weeks after the Allies invaded France it was quite clear to the Channel Island Group that nothing would be coming from the district which had provided them with supplies in the past. Thus it became obvious to them that they should return to Guernsey.

It became clear too, that in Guernsey, people would have to live on local produce and on the meagre contents of the stores. It was obvious that rationing would become even more severe and that much would depend on the resource-fulness of the Guernseyman who possessed land or any size of garden which could be used for the growing of vegetables, the keeping of rabbits etc. Unfortunately the German soldiers were so hungry that some of them took to begging and stealing which did not help the position.

The people of the Island who had no land were the ones faced with distress so the Controlling Committee, after consultation with Jersey, appealed to the Red Cross. As a result the "Vega" came to the Islands full of Red Cross parcels which were distributed to the people. The Germans made no attempt to upset arrangements and indeed assisted distribution.

This period of siege was a difficult time in which to sustain life and even the most privileged looked thin and haggard and their clothes left much to be desired.

There was no doubt that the parcels from the "Vega" had a great effect on the morale of the population and the day of Liberation brought such joy to the faces of the members of the populace that the effect was indescribable.

After all the official business of the Liberation was completed the British Government asked the Controlling Committee to stay in being for 90 days. Following this came an election to bring about a new States Assembly and Mr Falla was persuaded to stand as a deputy and to represent the parish of Torteval.

He served in this capacity for three years, an experience he has not forgotten, as the Douzaine of Torteval had to have the Billet explained in the Guernsey dialect.

At the next election Mr Falla stood for St Martin's and served this parish until he was elected Conseiller by which time he had served on many Committees including the Presidency of Horticulture, member and President of the Electricity Board, member and Vice President of the States Dairy, and member of the Advisory and Finance Committee.

In 1953 Mr Falla was elected President of Rotary, a presidency which he enjoyed very much. He became a Founder Member of the Royal Commonwealth Society of Guernsey, a Founder of the Guernsey Branch of the Commonwealth Parliamentary Association, and a Founder Member of the National Trust of Guernsey later becoming its President.

His next step was the founding of the Chest and Heart Association of which he is now the Patron. Continuing in his determination to help his fellow men he became a founder member of Guernsey's branch of the 'Workers Education Association' of which he is now President.

After the war Mr Falla represented Guernsey in the International Colorado Committee and was a founder Member of the European and Mediterranean Plant Health Organisation.

The pests brought into Europe during the War years had to be dealt with and this included the Colorado Beetle. One of the outstanding efforts of this Committee was to prevent the use of D.D.T. which did so much to harm the beneficial insects and birds.

After the War Mr Falla organised the import of the Dutch bulbs into Guernsey on a sound commecial basis, establishing an Arbitration Panel to settle disputes. The system operates to this day.

Continuing, Mr Falla mentioned his interest in the well being of French people living in Guernsey. He introduced this by mentioning that in the past the Island had liberally provided shelter to French people and being a fluent French speaker he helped after the War to reorganise the Roman Catholic Church in Guernsey, and the use of Victor Hugo's house in Hauteville. He took the view that Guernsey, having given shelter to this very notable Frenchman for fifteen years, his house should be maintained by the City of Paris and this indeed took place. On the occasion of the Centenary of the death of Victor Hugo the French visitors included the President of the French Republic, M. Francois Mitterand and the Mayor of Paris, M. Jacques Chirac.

Soon after the War the Guernsey Society for the Prevention of Cruelty to Animals called on Mr Falla to become its President and he was able to help them with the rehabilitation and renovation of their buildings.

Although nearly ninety years of age Mr Falla is still on the Boards of a number of Companies and there is no doubt that his success in attracting attention from so many organisations is connected with his undoubted intelligence, his enterprise, his linguistic powers and his ability to address audiences. In addition Mr Falla appears to possess the gift of dealing with worrying problems by attacking the centre of the problem rather than worrying about trivialities.

Because of his services to humanity Mr Falla was made a serving Brother of the Hospital of John of Jerusalem. He was also asked to act as a founder of the Cercle Francais along with the Canon E. L. Frossard and Mr Julius Touzeau, and Mr Falla received the Medaille D'argent de la Ville de Paris for preserving the French entity in Guernsey.

With regard to his work for horticulture he was awarded the 'H.R. Bichard Medal' and he served on the Committee of the 'Guernsey Growers Association'. In addition he became a member of the Plant Health Association and is a life member of the Farmers Club of London.

Of course, the O.B.E. presented by the Queen can be regarded as the crowning glory of his efforts to serve humanity.

May Mr Falla's efforts be copied by all and may he be with us for many more years.

Admiral The Right Hon. James Lord de Saumarez, G.C.B., K.S.

A very famous gentleman was born on the 11th March 1757 in the town of St Peter Port. He was a member of the renowned Guernsey family of de Saumarez which is of Norman extraction and of great antiquity in the Island. However during his Naval period James Saumarez was known simply as Saumarez and he was bearing this name when he entered the Navy in 1770 at the age of thirteen when he joined the Royal Navy and soon became a midshipman. In this rank he served on the Mediterranean station until 1775 when he returned home.

After a few weeks of rest James went to London to pass his examination as Lieutenant having spent the required six years in service.

In 1775 war broke out with the American colonies and James found himself on board the *Bristol* of 60 guns with a destination in South Carolina. Eventually the *Bristol* reached Charleston and James came under fire for the first time.

Lord Howe, Commander-in-Chief of the Fleet, selected James as his aide-de-camp and expressed his sincere thanks for the young Lieutenant's brave exertions. In 1778 James was appointed Lieutenant in command of the *Spitfire*, a schooner-rigged galley.

With the help of the other small ships an enemy frigate was captured and set on fire and James engaged the enemy 47 times, also helping in the defence at Rhode Island. Eventually two British ships and some small vessels stationed in a passage were burnt to prevent them from falling into strong enemy hands.

Subsequently seven hundred men who had been employed in the seize of Rhode Island were sent home in the *Leviathan* of fifty guns. Portsmouth was reached in 1779 and James was able to take a longed-for opportunity to visit his family.

Surely this was a sign that the American War of Independence would soon come to an end and in favour of America.

Admiral The Rt. Hon. James, Lord de Saumarez, G.C.B., K.S.,
General of Marines, 1757-1836.

James was next ordered to join the *Victory* as third Lieutenant but in 1781 when Admiral Hyde Parker joined the *Victory* he became first Lieutenant and later accompanied the Admiral to the *Fortitude* acting as first Lieutenant and participated in a battle with the Dutch Fleet which in the end proved indecisive.

On this occasion the young Saumarez was presented to his King who inquired whether he was related to the famous sailors Philip and Thomas Saumarez. The Admiral answered 'Yes please your Majesty, he is their Nephew and as brave and as good an officer as they were'. Saumarez was then promoted to Commander, (though only a second Lieutenant) and in 1791 was appointed to the command of the *Tisiphone*.

Commander Saumarez first served under Lord Howe in the Channel as a 'look out' and was able to spot the enemy. As a result of his work the Admiral pushed forward between a French convoy and captured twenty sail.

Commander Saumarez also distinguished himself by attacking and capturing a French ship of thirty-six guns and twenty-one sail were captured. They contained seven thousand seamen and several other ships struck their colours.

It was evident that a larger force of French ships than had been anticipated was being sent to capture Jamaica and Commander Saumarez was sent to inform Sir Samuel Hood of the position.

Actually he was able to deliver his dispatches to Captain Stanhope who ordered him to proceed to Antigua. It seemed impossible for Saumarez to communicate with Sir Samuel Hood, but he pushed through an intricate channel and by using care, skill and luck he navigated the *Tisiphone* to St Kitts and delivered his dispatches to Sir Samuel Hood.

Being in poor health Captain Stanhope was anxious to return to England, whereupon Captain Saumarez took over the *Russel*, Captain Stanhope's former command, and found that a formidable enemy fleet was standing to the North West. An order was given to set sail and when the weather made this possible, the engagement began. Captain Saumarez distinguished himself especially as he engaged the famous *Ville de Paris* and with assistance caused this ship to strike her colours. This was the "Battle of the Saints".

Captain Saumarez, still commanding the *Russel*, then sailed to England with 300 French seamen and 22 French officers all as prisoners.

The *Russel* was then paid off and Lord Howe confirmed Saumarez' commission to Post Captain. However, the part which he had played in the battle was unfortunately never recognised and others were given the credit so that Saumarez was unable to see any active service until 1793. He could however enjoy his family and our hero was greeted with great respect and affection in Guernsey.

H.M.S. St. Vincent *at Portsmouth. This ship represents a type used during the period when Lord de Saumarez served in the British Navy.*

When in Guernsey Captain Saumarez made his only visit to France, visiting Cherbourg to examine the Naval projects being developed which could at a later date become very dangerous to the Islands.

At length, the prospect of further war with France becoming obvious, Captain Saumarez was sent to the Channel Islands with the object of reinforcing the garrisons and protecting the convoys.

Early in 1793, while cruising off Cherbourg, Captain Saumarez, in the *Crescent*, a thirty-six gun vessel, attacked a

French vessel named *Le Reunion* which for some time had been a menace to English vessels.

The engagement lasted two hours and twenty minutes and although not a man was injured on board his ship, one hundred and twenty were either killed or injured on board his adversary. This exploit procured him the honour of Knighthood from the King and a handsome gift of a silver plate.

Sir James' next serious contact with the French took place when he was sent to investigate the rumour that preparations were being made by the French to invade the Islands.

Sir James set out from Plymouth with a small squadron to reconnoitre the strength of the enemy forces. He had three frigates *H.M.S. Crescent*, which was under his direct command, *H.M.S. Druid* and *H.M.S. Eurydice*.

Off the north-west of Guernsey he sighted two French ships of the line and three frigates making it practically certain that his force would be defeated. The *Eurydice*, being a slow sailer, was ordered to make for harbour around the south coast.

To prevent the capture of *Eurydice* Sir James with the *Druid* sailed in such a way as occasionally to engage the enemy thus giving the *Eurydice* a chance to reach a place of safety.

The French squadron gained upon both the *Crescent* and *Druid* and Sir James eventually decided that the capture of his own ship was inevitable unless he was able to develop an idea which came to his mind.

Being well acquainted with the coast himself and having on board an experienced pilot called Jean Breton, a native of the neighbouring coast, and a crew consisting largely of local characters, he determined to attempt a passage never before tried by a King's ship and having been given an assurance from Jean Breton that the passage was possible. Actually it turned out to be a narrow one consisting of avoiding rocks all the way until the frigate was conducted into the good roadstead of Guernsey to the great surprise and discomfort of the enemy who certainly had not deemed it prudent to follow the frigate.

As they went through the rocks Sir James asked Breton whether he was sure of his sea marks – "Quite sure Sir," replied the pilot "for there is my house and your house in line". It seems to me that Breton might just as well have said "It's all right, I do know what I'm doing".

Action off west coast of Guernsey, 8th June, 1794. Captain Sir James Saumarez,
H.M.S. Crescent, Druid and Euridice, Jean Breton, Pilot.

Again when the ship was still close enough to suffer from French cannon balls which were coming close to the frigate, Sir James is said to have drawn Breton's attention to the fact that he was ducking every time the cannon balls were coming near. In Guernsey French Sir James' remark would have been the following:- "Tu t'quette Breton" and the answer "Oui moussieu mais si vois perdae Breton vous perdae enne houmme". This translated would have been "Yes Sir, but if you lose Breton you lose a man". In fact Sir James would have lost his ship and his crew as everything depended on the skill of the pilot.

However gratified Sir James must have been at having succeeded in carrying out a masterly retreat from a much superior force, he must have been delighted to learn that Major-General Small, the Lieutenant-Governor of Guernsey and a large number of inhabitants had observed the whole of the naval evolutions from such observation posts as Le Guet at Cobo.

Immediately after the conclusion of the engagement the Governor published a most flattering testimonial of the gallant and distinguished conduct of Sir James Saumarez, his officers and men.

Route of Captain Sir James Saumarez' thrilling action along the west coast of Guernsey.

In addition, the Lieutenant-Governor presented John Breton with a silver gilt medal as a mark of the skill which he had displayed in the engagement. This was a large medal and it is now in the care of the Ancient Monuments Committee and will no doubt be on view in the Maritime Museum when it is completed.

According to James Marr, in 1793 Sir James Saumarez was engaged in a daring errand of mercy when he used five warships and ten transports to bring to Guernsey Roman Catholic refugees from the Jacobin Terror in France. It appears that these refugees were received with sympathy by the Islanders.

It would appear that the efficiency with which he discharged his duties played an important part in frustrating Napoleon's plans to invade not only the Channel Islands but Britain as well. While engaged in these operations Sir James destroyed a flotilla of enemy gunboats due to sail from Granville to the invasion assembly point at Boulogne.

Towards the end of 1794 Sir James Saumarez continued on the Channel fleet until his ship was taken to be recoppered. Sir James was then given a period of rest until he was successful in his application for the command of a battle ship. He was appointed to the *Orion* and attached to the Channel Fleet until he served under the orders of Sir John Jarvis, sometimes cruising in the Mediterranean and sometimes blockading the Port of Cadiz.

When off the Cape of St Vincent in February 1797 the Spanish fleet was seen and, although much larger in numbers of ships, this fleet was attacked by Sir John Jarvis and his fleet and four Spanish ships were captured. When fully considered there is little doubt that this action can be regarded as a British victory.

For the services rendered by the members of the *Orion's* crew, Sir James was presented with a gold medal and Sir John Jarvis eventually became Earl St Vincent, obviously connected with the battle of Cape St Vincent.

The subsequent blockade of Cadiz was almost entirely entrusted to Sir James and due to his vigilance no ships escaped.

Meanwhile Napoleon Bonaparte, at the head of a formidable fleet and army, was on his way to conquer Egypt. However, Earl St Vincent sent Rear Admiral Horatio Nelson with ships to oppose this move. These ships included the *Orion* under the command of Sir James Saumarez.

In spite of the small difficulties of the British ships the resultant victory was complete and Sir James Saumarez was instructed to take charge of the French prizes. This battle was subsequently referred to as "The Battle of the Nile". The *Orion* was taken back to England and arrived at Spithead where she remained until the end of the year.

In 1801 Sir James was honoured when he was presented for the second time with a gold medal and ribbon. In addition he also received the lucrative appointment of Colonel of Marines and was promoted to the Rank of Rear Admiral of the Blue and, in command of the *Caesar* with a Rear Admiral's Flag hoisted, Sir James Saumarez set sail to resume command of the inshore squadron off Brest so that not a single French ship escaped his vigilance. Eventually he received the order to end his fourteen week long cruise and on reaching Cowsand Bay he was informed in secret that he was to be sent with a squadron destined for an important service.

The Rear Admiral was given lengthy instructions marked "Most Secret" which indicated that he was to be sent to Cadiz where five Spanish ships of the line had arrived, so he was to take a squadron to prevent a single ship from leaving Cadiz. It was also mentioned that three Portuguese ships were being fitted out to assist in the task.

Finally the orders which the Rear-Admiral received mention that Napoleon Bonaparte was expected in Cadiz and that the ships then arming in Cadiz were to be commanded by French officers.

Before he left for his new assignment, His Majesty, having realised the meritorious services of Sir James, created him a Baronet and he was authorised to wear the supporters and arms of his family which had been registered in the Heralds' Office since the reign of Charles II.

The ships of the new squadron cleared the English Channel and crossed the Bay of Biscay and eventually cruised off Cadiz and little happened until intelligence was received that three French ships of the line and a frigate had anchored off Algeciras. The Admiral decided to attack these ships but the attempt was not successful. French losses were high – 306 killed and nearly 500 wounded whilst the British losses were 123 killed and 240 wounded.

The crippled squadron was received warmly in Gibraltar. Efforts were made to repair the damaged ships, to attend to the wounded in the hospital in Gibraltar and to do everything possible for those taken as prisoners, who were reported to have been rather badly treated in the hospital at Algeciras. Everything was done to repair the damaged ships and in fact they were repaired in five days and again sought the enemy whose force had been nearly tripled by the addition of six ships of the line and three frigates from Cadiz.

On the 12th July 1801 the British squadron were engaged in another conflict with the French and Spanish ships. This resulted in a British victory to the delight of the people of Gibraltar. Sir James' efforts were fully acknowledged, but not fully rewarded, although after a lapse of several months he received the thanks of both Houses of Parliament and every large Corporation and his reward was the red riband of the Order of the Bath.

For a while Sir James continued with the squadron employed on the blockade of Cadiz. However, this was disturbed by news of great successes which included the surrender of Alexandria and Cairo, and the final expulsion of the French from Egypt. This aroused great rejoicing in Gibraltar as did the news that Admiral Saumarez was to be honoured with the Order of the Bath with riband and star.

The result was a grand procession in Gibraltar which involved representatives of the Navy, Royal Artillery, dignitaries of Gibraltar including the Governor, the Admiral's secretary bearing on a cushion the Insignia of the Order of the Bath, and then Admiral Sir James Saumarez himself supported by many officers of the Royal Navy and one of the three bands involved.

Eventually Sir James remained in Gibraltar until his return to land where he was to be presented with a sword and the Freedom of London. The Island of Guernsey also presented him with a handsome piece of silver.

Hostilities with France seemed likely to be resumed and on the 11th March 1803 Sir James hoisted his flag at Sheerness on board the *Zealand*. His squadron consisted of six frigates and cutters which were employed in blockading the French coast. A flotilla of armed vessels assembled at Granville were heavily bombarded by the Admiral. Subsequently it was revealed that the French flotilla was so damaged that any action on their part would be delayed until the end of the year. The Admiral continued his blockade and the Channel Islands were given more time to put themselves into a state of defence.

During the year 1806 the enemy convoys were responsible for the victualling of the considerably increased French fleet at Brest and the squadron under Sir James was actively employed in intercepting these convoys.

When possible, Sir James was happy seeing his family and friends in Guernsey but he was also pleased to establish and support useful institutions in the Island.

Early in 1807 Earl St Vincent was appointed to command the Channel Fleet. He immediately asked for Saumarez to be second in command who being promoted to the rank of Vice Admiral hoisted his flag on board the *Prince of Wales* which, captured in 1782, had been constantly employed ever since. Unfortunately Sir James was displaced and consequently asked to be superseded and in February 1808 he proceeded to Guernsey.

In the meantime war with Russia broke out and it became evident that the Baltic must soon become the seat of war. Of the countries of Northern Europe, Sweden alone remained friendly but Russian preparations for an invasion of Sweden alarmed King Gustavus Adolphus who sent the most earnest appeals for a large naval and military force to be sent from England for the protection of his country.

The *Victory*, thoroughly repaired after Trafalgar, was commissioned for the use of Sir James who had been selected to act as Commander in Chief with Rear Admirals under his command, and the ships composing the fleet preceded an army expedition of 10,000 troops to increase the British support of Sweden.

The Russians laid siege on an important fort and the Commander surrendered which led not only to the loss in Sweden's war against Russia but also caused the loss of Finland as a supporter of Sweden.

However, in the presence of British forces the enemy was prevented from entering into Sweden. Although Sir James's fleet was then opposed by Russians, Prussians, French, Danes and Norwegians, Sir James maintained his forces so that they were judiciously disposed. Little did he know that he would maintain this position for five years in the Baltic and this he

119

did by affording communications by sea to the Russians who had become British Allies. Such a privilege was of course denied to the French and indeed every effort was made to help to bring about Napoleon's downfall.

James's duties were very largely diplomatic and he proved to have a great influence over events and decisions occuring in Sweden which he was able to steer in Britain's favour.

In return for his valuable service the Grand Cross of the Honourable Military Order of the Sword was conferred on him by King Charles the Thirteenth of Sweden on his accession to the throne.

Sir James continued in this status until 1812 and before he left he received a superb sword from the King of Sweden, the hilt being set with brilliants and displaying exquisite workmanship.

Sir James Saumarez, when in Guernsey, made generous donations to local charities, towards the improvement of the Castel and St Andrew's schools and without publicity he helped many of those in need.

Sir James also conceived the idea of providing a Church where the services would be in English thus improving the relationships between the Garrison and the Islanders – a

Lord de Saumarez's monument at Delancey Park.

project which came to fruition when St James the Less was constructed. In the same way Sir James founded the Guernsey Savings Bank, now absorbed into the Trustees Savings Bank.

It appears that contingents of the Swedish Navy visited the Island on two occasions, in 1910 and 1926. On each occasion they laid wreaths on Lord de Saumarez's monument at Delancey Park. Accompanying the wreaths they brought beautiful large silk ribbons of blue and gold on which were inscribed the following:-

1910 To the memory of Vice-Admiral, Lord de Saumarez, noble in Rank as he was in mind.

1926 A tribute of admiration and gratitude to the memory of Vice-Admiral Lord de Saumarez – Commander-in-Chief of the Baltic 1808 to 1812. Nothing could shake his confidence in the Swedes.

These tributes placed in suitable containers having a glass front were attached to the wall of the Royal Court where they could be seen by anyone having business in the Court Room.

After the alterations were concluded in the Court the containers containing the Swedish tributes were removed to Saumarez Park where they can be seen today to be properly exhibited.

In addition, on the 4th September 1975, a commemorative plaque to Lord de Saumarez was unveiled in Gothenburg City Hall in the presence of H.M. the King of Sweden and the Earl Mountbatten of Burma. This again shows how real was the gratitude of the Swedes for the success (mainly diplomatic) which had been achieved by Lord de Saumarez at a time when Europe was cursed with wars.

The visit in 1990 of the Swedish Ambassador from London demonstrated once more the respect of the Swedes for the work done by Lord de Saumarez in their country so many years ago.

It would be very desirable if an attractive memorial to Lord de Saumarez could be seen replacing the one destroyed by the German Forces, when the next Swedish visitors come to Guernsey.

Summary of Important Events connected with Lord de Saumarez

1770 At the age of 13 years joined the Royal Navy as midshipman.

1778 After attack of Charleston promoted Lieutenant.

1781 After Dogger Bank incident promoted to Second Lieutenant

1781 After bravery shown in dreadful sea fight made Commander and presented to the King as Captain Saumarez.

1785 Married Miss Martha Le Marchant.

1793 Received honour of Knighthood and presented with a piece of plate by merchants of London after capturing French 36 gun ship *Reunion* without any of his men being hurt.

1799 Appointed Colonel of Marines.

1801 Created a Baronet. Awarded Star and ribbon of the Bath. Received Freedom of City of London and a handsome sword, whilst guns of the Park and Tower of the City of London were fired. Promoted to Rear-Admiral of the Blue. Presented with silver vase from inhabitants of Guernsey.

1808 Period on diplomatic duties in Sweden where he was presented with Grand Cross of the Military Order of the Sword.

1812 On leaving Sweden he was awarded a superb Sword by the King of Sweden set with brilliants and of exquisite workmanship.

1814 Sir James was promoted to Admiral of the Blue.

1824 Appointed Port Admiral of Plymouth and General of Marines.

1831 Created a peer of the United Kingdom – his title being Baron de Saumarez of Guernsey.

1834 Elected an Elder Brother of Trinity House.
      Received a full portrait of the King of Sweden – sent by the King himself.

1836 Death of Lord de Saumarez – 1,000 persons reputed to have attended interment at Castel cemetery. Muffled bells were heard all over Island as well as gun fire from Castle Cornet and Fort George.

Onwards – Island wide collection brought about the erection of a magnificent memorial at Delancey Park which was destroyed by German Forces during the Second World War. Fortunately the bronze plaques depicting a bust of the Admiral, some of his naval triumphs and his action off Guernsey in 1794 were preserved in the care of the Ancient Monuments Committee.

Lieutenant-General Sir John Doyle, Baronet, G.C.B., K.C.

LIEUTENANT General Sir John Doyle was a most popular Lieutenant Governor of Guernsey who was appointed to this most important Island post after distinguishing himself fighting for Britain when the Americans succeeded in gaining their independence from Britain.

This war at an end Brigade Major Doyle was then elected to the Irish Parliament but relatively soon afterwards he found himself involved in the wars with France where his performance was such that he earned sufficient renown to be promoted to the rank of Lieutenant General and in 1803 he was sent to Guernsey as Lieutenant Governor when the Island was in serious danger of being invaded by the French.

Doyle commenced his work in Guernsey by improving the performance of the Militia seeing that it was improved and better trained. Without any great difficulty he persuaded the States of Guernsey to vote £30,000 for supplies for his plan which embraced the improvement of the defences of the entire coast from La Salerie in an anti-clockwise direction to Fermain Bay, the defence of St Peter Port being left to Castle Cornet and the uncompleted Fort George.

Doyle planned that every vantage point from La Salerie to Grand Havre was to be used to accommodate a battery of guns and from Grand Havre to Grandes Rocques the bays were to have batteries of guns whose fortifications were to be supplemented by powder magazines.

Further down the west coast parapets were to be built at the Houmet peninsular and L'Eree and battery sites constructed while the ancient "Rocquaine Castle" (Fort Grey) was to be repaired and guns placed at strategic points on the rising ground above the bays.

Finally the old "Castle" at Pezeries Point was to be repaired, the parapets strengthened and a powder magazine installed.

Although it was obvious that the cliffs would provide natural

Lieutenant-General Sir John Doyle, Baronet, G.C.B., K.C.

125

defenses Doyle insisted on the erection of watch houses at the high points such as La Prevoté, Les Tielles, Mon Herault and Pleinmont.

The vulnerable bays of Petit Bot, Saints and Fermain had also to be dealt with and Doyle asked for the erection of ramparts of stone at least 12 feet high supplemented by trenches and parapets whilst batteries also had to be built on the cliffs.

Having dealt with the primary defence Doyle turned his attention to communications so as to ensure that the movement of troops and guns would not be impaired.

To reach the newly accessible Clos du Valle, Doyle built a military road, "La Route Militaire". This road ran from the east coast road beginning at a spot now known as Halfway and carried on to the Vale Church.

Another military road followed running from Belle Greve Bay and Grande Maison Road to St Sampson's Bridge. Later it was continued along Vale Avenue turning left into Braye Road and extending to Camp du Roi and Landes du Marché.

The sections of these roads which are built on reclaimed land with no previous roads to follow are notable for their extreme straightness and most of Doyle's roads were planned to have a main carriageway of satisfactory width and a footpath four feet wide. What a benefit it would be if all our country roads were built like this especially when one considers the width of some of the vehicles now used all over Guernsey.

The Vazon Road ran via Les Gravees, the Castel Church and La Houguette to the coast at Vazon Tower whilst the Rocquaine Road ran by way of Fort George, Saumarez Manor, St Martin's Rectory, Le Bourg and Les Paysans Road to L'Eree. The construction of these two roads alone, totalling 11 miles in length involved the purchase of 12 vergees of additional land and the bringing in of 35,200 cart-loads of hardcore.

In 1812 the existing military roads were linked together by a road from the Longstore to St Martin's via Amherst, Queen's Road, Mount Row, Ville au Roi and Les Merriennes. Eventually a road from Mount Row led straight into the wilds of the Hougue Fouque where the emergency gun could be fired and the Island placed under martial law.

In 1913 the route which we call Cobo Road was built from the bottom of Rohais as far as La Planque near Saumarez

Original Memorial to Sir John Doyle, erected at Jerbourg.

Park and the following year again a road was built from La Planque crossing the road to Vazon at La Houguette and continuing via King's Mills, Le Mont Saint and Les Rouvets to join the Rocquaine road near L'Eree.

During his term of office John Doyle was created a Baronet in 1805 and was also elected to the Parliament of the United Kingdom as Member for Newport, Isle of Wight, holding this seat for the two years 1806 and 1807.

By the time of Napoleon's defeat Guernsey's Lieutenant-Governor had attained tremendous popularity and his recall in 1816 took place in spite of emphatic remonstrances by the States which urged his retention in office although in fact he had been technically subordinate from 1807 to the Earl of Pembroke who became Governor in 1807 whilst Sir John was effectively at the helm.

In 1826 he visited Guernsey and came ashore to be treated with a rapturous welcome. He disembarked at the St Julian Rock and here the waiting Islanders took the horses out of the carriage that awaited him and hauled it in triumph to the Town.

Sir John Doyle died in London in 1834 but this great man has never been forgotten in the Bailiwick where his memory is perpetuated by a road, two forts (one in Guernsey and the other in Alderney) a sea passage and a group of dwellings at L'Ancresse on the site of the barracks that he had established. However it was the column at Jerbourg erected in his memory which always received the most attention. Although destroyed by the Germans in the Second World War, it has since been replaced by a commemorative obelisk.

Major General Sir Isaac Brock, K.B.

ON October 13th, 1769 a week old baby was taken to the Town Church to be christened. He was Isaac Brock and his parents were John Brock and Elizabeth de Lisle. Surprising as it may be the baby was their eleventh child and eighth son and subsequently there were three more christenings bringing the total to fourteen children.

This very large family eventually lived at the top of High Street in a building now occupied by "Boots the Chemists". Actually at this time it was common place to have large families and parents considered themselves lucky if half their children survived.

No one present at that christening could have foretold that this baby boy would lay down his life in the act of earning the title of "The Hero of Upper Canada" by defending and saving the whole Dominion from successful invasion by the forces of the United States of America.

Isaac Brock is said to have been more interested in sport than in his school work. He fished, sailed, rode horses and played games. His father died when he was 8 years old and at the age of 11 he was sent away to boarding schools, first at Southampton and then at Rotterdam.

Away from home Isaac proved to be a good scholar, he developed a love of reading and was fluent in French. Isaac's ambition was to be a soldier and he had no difficulty in achieving this object as the British were at war almost continuously all through the 18th century.

At the age of fifteen years Isaac Brock entered the army by purchase as an ensign in the 8th Regiment of Foot and then transferred to the 49th (later the Royal Berkshires) in which he rose with unusual rapidity to the rank of Lieutenant-Colonel at the age of twenty eight. He was tall having been six feet and two inches in height at the age of twenty one and furthermore he was a good looking man.

In 1797 as a Lieutenant-Colonel Isaac fought in the 59th Foot in Holland and the regiment under his command distinguished itself. Four years later in 1801 he enhances his repu-

Queenston Heights Statue in memory of Major-General Brock.

130

tation by his bearing in Admiral Nelson's attack on Copenhagen where he was second in command of the land forces.

Lieutenant-Colonel Brock also served in England at the regiment's depot recruiting and training young soldiers to be sent to join the regiments in Barbados. It is not likely that he spent much time in Guernsey apart from holidays from his school in England and occasional army leaves.

He is reported as being bitterly disappointed when his regiment was ordered to Canada away from all chances of active service against Napoleon in Europe. However he must have gained some satisfaction at being promoted to full Colonel.

However when he arrived in the New World, he dealt promptly and efficiently with a crisis, rapidly suppressing a conspiracy organised by deserters.

In 1805 Brock came home on leave during which he is reported as having spent a delightful time with relatives and friends. However when relations with the United States of America deteriorated in 1806 he was hurriedly recalled to Canada.

Shortly after his arrival in Canada he was made a Brigadier and in 1810 he was given command of Upper Canada as well as being appointed as provisional Lieutenant-Governor of the Province in command of all the British Troops in that country.

What really worried Brock was the very long frontier with the United States of America as at this time trouble was arising between the British and the Americans of the United States.

Eventually he was quartered at Quebec where he repaired the old fortifications, built a military hospital and made a parade ground for the troops but he was particularly anxious about the safety of Queenston on the Niagara River below the falls where a force could so easily make a crossing.

It was in 1811 when the United States had declared war on Canada that it fell upon Canada to fight the battle of the British Empire: a battle which the American's Secretary for War maintained was going to be a War that could be won without soldiers.

However when raising a militia Brock had enrolled a large number of wonderful men who had left their homes, farms etc in the United States and moved into Canada simply because they wanted to remain British and were called "United Empire Loyalists".

When the Americans actually invaded Canada with 15,000 men Brock was appointed Major General in Command of a small force of 1,500 men to which he was able to persuade some friendly Red Indians to join. The first successful encounter with the enemy was centred on Sault St Mary and this success settled any doubt that existed in the minds of the Red Indians and many threw in their lot with the British force, and Brock found that Tecumseh an Indian Brave was a born soldier and a born diplomatist.

The next great success for the British was the capture of Detroit, the Red Indians being asked by General Brock not

Plaque on one side of memorial on Queenston Heights.

132

Memorial at Brockville.

133

to use their scalping knives on the vanquished and it is pleasing to be able to record that the Red Indians kept faithfully to the no knives request. Actually this success has been regarded by the Canadians as Brock's most brilliant exploit.

The Americans were furious at these disasters and they were expected to make another attempt to defeat the British. This was known to General Brock and he decided that the most likely place for this attack would be at Niagara and sure enough the boom of guns was eventually heard coming from this region.

Immediately General Brock mounted his grey charger and he galloped hard till he came to the residence of Capt. Powell where without dismounting he took a cup of coffee from the hands of General Shaw's daughter to whom he was engaged.

General Brock had been assured that the Americans could not possibly climb the three hundred feet of cliff which rose almost sheer from the river. Suddenly however there was a crash of musketry and American troops were seen at the top of the hill. They had indeed found a method of avoiding the cliff and climbing the hill.

The British contingent then tackled the long and arduous climb to the top of the hill and nearing the top, Brock fell, shot through the breast at close quarters and when the news was circulated the whole Empire mourned his loss at a time when everyone was elated with the victory achieved at Queenston Heights.

Upper Canada dedicated a monument on Queenston Heights to the memory of Lieut Major-General Sir Isaac Brock K.B. — Provisional Lieut. Governor and Commander of the Forces in the Province. Under this monument it is reported that the remains of the dead man were deposited in a suitable vault. He fell in action near these heights on the thirteenth day of October 1812 in the 43rd year of his age — revered and lamented by the people whom he had governed and deplored by the Sovereign in whose service his life had been devoted.

In Guernsey a plaque exists on the "Boots" building to inform the public that this was the house in which Sir Isaac lived in his youth. The exact wording is the following "Major General Isaac Brock K.B. who saved Canada for the Empire

Major-General Sir Isaac Brock, K.B.

lived here. He was born in 1769 and was killed in action in 1812".

In addition the Brock Memorial Chapel is to be found in the Town Church and a plaque can be found on the outside wall of the Church fixed off the east side of the main entrance. This plaque should certainly be seen with pride as it was brought over from Canada by the Agent General from Ontario. The occasion of the unveiling represented the 200th Anniversary of the birth of Major-General Sir Isaac Brock K.B. who was then described as the President and Administrator of Upper Canada (now Ontario).

The costs of the plaque etc were borne by the Ontario Archaeological and Historical Sites Board of the Department of Tourism and Information.

Attending at the unveiling were the Lieutenant-Governor Sir Charles Mills, the Bailiff — Sir William Arnold and Lady Mills. In addition many other prominent Islanders had been invited and attended the reception which followed.

Other memorials include the one to be seen in Ontario conveyed there by Sir William Arnold Kt, C.B.E., K.St.J., L.L.D. and Lady Arnold also to commemorate the 200th Anniversary of our hero's birth.

Other expressions of the gratitude felt for Major-General Brock's devotion to his duty to the Canadian People as well as to his Sovereign can be seen in the following:—
A memorial in St Paul's Cathedral.
A Bust erected outside the Brock-ville Court House as well as the naming of the town itself as Brock-ville.
The Brock University in Ontario and the Brock Centre for the Arts at the University.
The Upper Canada's Memorial to Sir Isaac Brock, K.B.

The following also deserve inclusion:—
Brock Road in St Peter Port and
Brock Road in St Sampson's.

136

Nurse, Lieutenant George Edward, V.C. (1873-1945)

A valiant Castel resident

GEORGE Edward Nurse was born on April 14th, 1873, to Jane (neé Benfon), the wife of Charles Nurse, who in 1879 (when he bought it from Amos Chick) became the owner of Cobo Hotel — an establishment which, prior to the destruction of the building by the Germans during the Occupation, stood at the junction of La Banquette and La Neuve Route.

The lad grew up in this hostelry in the Castel and received his primary education at the Chamberlain Academy (a private kindergarten in Victoria Road), whence he went on to the Boys' Intermediate School as one of the first pupils in attendance after its initial opening at its original home of Granville House, Mount Durand in 1883.

On leaving school George Nurse was apprenticed to Mr H. R. Hansford, a farrier whose business was located in Havilland Street, and on January 6th, 1892, he enlisted at Saint George's Barracks, London, to ply this trade in the Royal Field Artillery. He remained in service until his transfer to the reserve in 1898 and spent four years at Ladysmith in the British Colony of Natal and eventually returned to Guernsey early in 1899.

Three months later, however, the worsening situation in South Africa culminated in the outbreak of war on October 12th. This led to his being recalled to the colours — and before long he found himself back in Natal where he had sailed from England on the S.S. "Dunottar Castle".

George then fought throughout the Boer campaign, from Durban in the east to the relief of Mafeking in the west of the country. In the course of these operations, as part of an abortive attempt made on December 15th, 1899, to relieve Ladysmith — the British garrison which was besieged by the foe — the Sixth Infantry Brigade was ordered to cross the Tugela River by means of the bridge in the Village of Colenso, with the Brigade's artillery which included the 66 Field

Lieut. Nurse wearing V.C.

138

Battery, commanded by Major W. Foster, in which Nurse was serving as a Corporal.

This brigade included a battery of six Naval 12-pounders which were deployed forward to engage the Boer positions at a range of one thousand yards. The expected infantry attack failing to materialize and their guns (which had no shields) running short of ammunition, the gunners were withdrawn to cover of a deep-sided ravine (a "donga" in South African parlance) five hundred yards in the rear, in order to prevent a continuance of the heavy casualties being inflicted on them while they remained exposed to Afrikaner marksmen.

Shortly afterwards, however, General Sir Redvers Henry Buller, V.C. (at that time Commander-in-Chief of the Expeditionary Force and who, coincidentally, had also travelled from England on the "Dunottar Castle") arrived on the scene and, seeing these guns apparently abandoned, ordered their recovery. This order was implemented under withering enemy fire. Butler's three ADC's Captain Schofield, Captain Congreve and Lieutenant Roberts volunteered for the tasks. The intensity of the fire between the donga and the artillery pieces was such that one of the dead was later found to have been hit no less than sixty-four times. This murderous fusillade resulted in a mere two out of the six guns involved being retrieved — and it was in achieving this limited (though costly) success that the Old Intermedian played so conspicuous a part.

With great courage the intrepid N.C.O. managed to secure a few loose horses and while Lieutenant the Honourable Frederick Roberts held his horse for him, he hooked the others to some limbers. Scorning a merciless hail of raking shot, subaltern and Corporal, together with other audacious volunteers, then set out across those terrible five hundred yards towards the guns the recovery of which was required, the perils confronting them being dramatically evoked in Nurse's personal recollections:

"The bullets were pattering around us like hail. One went through my haversack, piercing a hand-glass and a piece of bread I had in it, hit my revolver pouch and splintered one of the fingers of my right hand in two places".

As they rushed forward Lieutenant Roberts fell mortally wounded but his companion continued undaunted and with the help of Captain Harry Schofield, limbered up two of the guns which were then hauled away. Subsequent to the engagement Nurse himself — as recounted by Sir O'Moore Graig, V.C., in his authoritative compilation, "The V.C. and the D.S.C." — described in these words his deeds on that momentous day:

"I got hold of some loose horses and hooked them into the limbers, Lieutenant Roberts holding my horse meanwhile. Just after we started Lieutenant Roberts was shot. When we got to the guns, through a tornado of rifle bullet and shell. One gun had the spade clamping gear jammed and so I ran to another gun and with Captain Schofield's help limbered it up, then ran back to the former gun, found the pin, and managed to limber it up myself. When we were out of bullet-

Guns at Colenso.

140

range, I met Captain Reed and four teams on their way to attempt the recovery of more guns but they were bowled over at the drift at 500 yards' range."

For their valour in this action Major William (later Major-General Sir William) Babtie, Captains Hamilton Lyster Reed, Walter Norris Congreve and Harry Norton Schofield, together with Lieutenant the Honourable Frederick Hugh Sherston Roberts (the only son of Field Marshal Baron Roberts of Kandahar, V.C. — later Earl Roberts — who the next month replaced General Buller as Commander-in-Chief) and Corporal George Edward Nurse (who was promoted to Sergeant immediately after his courageous exploit) were awarded the Victoria Cross: the fifth-named posthumously. The Guernsey-man's award was gazetted on February 2nd, 1900. The Victoria Cross is the highest British award for bravery awarded to members of the British Forces. It was instituted by Queen Victoria and could be awarded to all ranks of the three services.

On October 10th, 1900, the 66 Battery was being transported by rail when the train, while crossing the Kaaf River, jumped the lines. In the resultant crash three men were killed and fifteen injured, while upwards of fifty horses were also either killed or injured. Nurse received fractures of the ribs and chest — injuries which led to his being invalided back to the United Kingdom where he was admitted to Netley Hospital. On discharge from hospital he crossed to Guernsey, sailing from Weymouth on the S.S. "Gazelle" and landed at the White Rock at 7 a.m. on Thursday, February 7th, 1901. Here he was greeted by his old employer, Mr H. R. Hansford, and the Headmaster of the Intermediate School, Mr William Sharp, together with an assemblage of the school's pupils and Old Boys. The horses were removed from the shafts of the carriage awaiting him and a group of exultant schoolboys dragged it jubilantly along Saint Julian's Pier as far as the Weighbridge — where the horses were put back between the shafts for the triumphal drive to Cobo. The absence of any civic reception by island dignitaries at the Harbour was rather weakly justified by pleading as its cause insufficient notice of the hero's arrival — but it is hard to avoid suspecting that the gallant Sergeant's somewhat lowly social status more likely accounted for his return home being denied official recognition. Such were the prejudices of the age — although it must be admitted

141

that in this case there is a further possible explanation for what at first sight seems a contemptible snub.

Thus George Nurse V.C. returned to his family but after the end of hostilities in South Africa he decided to stay in the Royal Artillary and subsequently he served during the Great War of 1914-1918. The former Corporal steadily rose in rank at a time when class distinction was strong. Thus on the 15th September he was made a temporary Second Lieutenant and then Lieutenant on 1st July, 1917.

George Nurse remained a lieutenant until April 1919 when he retired at the end of a long and distinguished career.

George's father Charles had bought a cottage at Route de Carteret, Cobo, which he named Colenso after George was awarded the V.C. but the cottage was sold in 1915 after Charles died.

George and his family visited Guernsey and stayed at Cobo Inn which was situated at the junction of La Banquette, La Neuve Route and the Coast Road to Cobo. However the inn was sold to George Robilliard by Mrs Nurse's heirs on her death and became a private dwelling.

Curiously enough in Guernsey George Nurse was referred to as Captain Nurse but it has been impossible to discover the reason for the apparent rise in rank. Indeed it is known that George went to America on some mission and it may be that his very great knowledge of guns had been of special value to the Americans.

Assuming that this mission had been arranged by British Authorities this may account for the elevation to Captain. Otherwise it may just have been a local addition of no significance.

A person who met George when he was 57 years old noted that his appearance belied his age and that he was extremely diffident about his honours. In fact there were many of the staff with whom he worked at Custom House who did not know that they harboured a V.C in their midst.

George Nurse had married Kathleen Meagher and they had one son Charles P. Colenso Nurse who was called Colenso by the family.

During the Occupation the Germans found it necessary to destroy the inn, the stables etc at Cobo so that no trace remains of the Cobo Inn.

George Nurse died on 25 November, 1945. His Victoria Cross is now owned by 159 (Colenso) Field Battery Royal Artillery, the modern day successors to 66 Field Battery.

I wish to thank Mr L. James Marr for assistance in preparing this article.

Lavoirs still used by French women

IT was the Protected Buildings Officer of the Ancient Monuments Committee who telephoned me to ask whether I would investigate the condition of a "Douit des Laveresse" at the Kings Mills which had been closed for many years.

This I agreed to do adding that I felt sure that Mr George Bramall would agree to join in the investigation and I was extremely pleased when this prediction came to pass.

First of all we examined the stone wall forming the southern face of the wall in the bend of the road which leads from the Kings Mills to Le Gele. We were of course searching for the old entrance to the stream, which carries water to Vazon Bay and we eventually found it and this led us to use George's ladder to look over the wall in the hope of finding evidence of the stone-work associated with a "Lavoir" and this we saw quite clearly.

We then went to see Mr L. G. Dorey of "Brooklands" who helped us a very great deal lending us a long ladder to

enable us to peer over the wall of the Stream or Douit which runs alongside his property. From here we could see further evidence of the presence of the old "Lavoir" but what we were searching for was a method of actually examining the "Lavoir" at close quarters and here we were greatly helped by Mr Dorey who led us to a door which opened on to the "Douit", but unfortunately to reach our goal we would have had to pass under several concrete buttresses which cross over the stream.

Our next aim was to avoid these concrete buttresses and with this in mind I interviewed the other close neighbour, Advocate N. J. M. Tostevin, who kindly allowed us to pass over his property in order to examine the "Lavoir". The Advocate's property was used at first for inspection and then

afterwards with the help of Mr Bramall's invaluable ladder we descended to the bed of the stream armed with the necessary tools to clear the "Lavoir" of vegetation.

This was the end of our efforts as we discovered that the "Lavoir" could be restored at relatively little cost and that the approach from the road could also be easily restored. Here Mr Bramall suggested the installation of a "Grille" in the wall to enable people to see it from the road.

Finally as we left the site Mr Dorey mentioned that formerly there was a dam across the stream a little below the Lavoir site. This enabled a "build up" of water for those washing their clothes. Mr Dorey also mentioned that at one time a pipe drew water from this place and under pressure this water was able to turn apparatus used for butter making and then the pipe finally emptied itself at a lower level into the stream.

Mr Bramall then produced a photograph taken on a visit to France. The scene was photographed in a recent visit to a village near Falaise and shows a lady washing her clothes in a "Lavoir".

Certainly the French have the reputation of using "Lavoirs" for the essential task of washing clothes. It appears that William the Conqueror's father first saw a tanner's daughter at Falaise "Lavoir" washing linen and fell in love with her.

Curiously enough my father always associated "the Lavoir" at the foot of Prince Albert's Road, St Peter Port with French women and I believe it was still being used in the early part of the present century.

Subsequent to this Mr Carol Toms kindly offered me a number of photographs showing French women using "Lavoirs" to wash their clothes. It would appear that the majority of these photographs were taken fairly recently in France except for two which were taken by Mr Charles H. Toms at the beginning of this century showing French women washing clothes in the "Lavoir" situated at the foot of Prince Albert's Road, St Peter Port.

Castle Cornet at War
Escape in the nick of time

DURING the Civil War Guernsey held out for Cromwell and the Parliamentary side whilst Castle Cornet supported the King (Charles I). This meant that the Castle was virtually at war with the Island and the eight long years during which the siege lasted it is estimated that 10,000 cannon balls were fired at the Town causing considerable damage to property and injuries to the inhabitants.

The siege ended when the Castle capitulated being the last Royalist Castle to do so.

In recognition of the gallant resistance to the Parliamentary forces it was agreed that the officers and soldiers would be allowed to leave the Castle carrying their arms, displaying their ensigns, bullets in their mouths and match lit at both ends. Having reached the Island they then had to lay down their arms except the officers who were allowed to keep their swords and some of their pistols.

At the beginning of the siege efforts had been made by the King's men who occupied the Castle to bring about a change of sympathy in the Island from Parliament to King and the following dramatic incident is an example of the atmosphere of the times.

In October 1643 Captain Bowden who was believed to be a staunch Parliamentary supporter brought his ship to a position off Fermain Bay and sent his long-boat with a letter for the Lieut-Governor and the three Commissioners who were the virtual rulers of the Island acting for the Parliamentary rulers of Britain.

The letter explained that Captain Bowden wished to discuss important matters with the Commissioners and after some hesitation three Commissioners Pierre de Beauvoir, James de Havilland and Pierre Carey went on board the ship only to realise that Captain Bowden had become a supporter of the King and that they had been tricked into coming to the ship.

148

Two of the King's Officers were present and tried to persuade the Commissioners to surrender the Island to the King — an action which they strongly refused to consider.

Eventually the three Commissioners were transferred to Castle Cornet where they were met by a guard of 50 men and taken to a damp, dark dungeon. However the next day they were moved to the room above the dungeon which proved to be an improvement but the food and sleeping arrangements left much to be desired.

The Civil War: 'The Escape from Castle Cornet' (1643).

After a period of six weeks the three prisoners decided to escape. Of course there was no fine pier as at present but a rough causeway similar to that at Lihou Island, which could only be used at periods of very low tide.

The first action to be taken was to cut a hole in the floor of their prison in order to reach some flax with which they could make some rope.

This hole was made by using knives to cut the required aperture and after four days the task was accomplished and everything given a normal appearance. This hole made it possible to draw up 14 or 15 parcels of flax which were made into the three different lengths of rope considered necessary in order to descend down the walls on to the rocks below.

They then had to choose a time when the visability would

149

not be too good, when the sentries were busy elsewhere and when the tide would be at its lowest so that they could scramble over the rocks and pebbles leading to the causeway.

It was in the beginning of December 1643 they took the first step by tying a rope to a pillar in their room. From here they descended to the room below using their hole and here Mr de Havilland smashed the door lock with an iron bar.

They then went to the gun facing west and tied a rope to it but just as they were going to slide down they saw three guards on duty below. They quickly passed to another gun on the south side of the Castle from where they slid down the first and second walls.

When on the rocky area below they made all speed towards the causeway but unfortunately just as they reached the causeway they were seen and the shout was heard — "Fire — Fire! the prisoners are running away".

Fortunately some little time was necessary before the soldiers could load their weapons and the most important gun misfired a number of times so that this gave a chance to the three men to reach comparative safety where although shots fell around them they were not hit.

When they reached the end of the causeway the people who saw them ran to the Church and spread the news so that the congregation emerged to welcome the Commissioners with cheers and shouts of joy.

Sometime later news reached the inhabitants that had the Commissioners remained half an hour more in the Castle they would have been hanged as the order for this action had already been received by Sir Peter Osborne the Royalist Governor of the Castle.

The Church in Guernsey at the Reformation

UNTIL the Reformation the services in the Island churches were almost certainly held in the Latin language. After the Reformation, until the beginning of the twentieth century, the French language was used, but the greatest difference occurred in the teachings and practices of the two sides, Catholic and Protestant.

The Catholic Faith taught belief in the state of Purgatory, where the souls of the dead remained until judged fit for heaven, or were condemned to hell. It was also believed that the dead could be helped by praying to the saints on their behalf, and the saints would then intervene with God who would then cut short the time spent in Purgatory.

At this time also, the Church encouraged its members to leave sums of money in wills or as gifts, so that special services (Masses) could be said by the priests on behalf of the dead parishioner, or indeed on behalf of a living person or a whole family.

This urge to pray for the living and the dead led to the setting up of Chantry Chapels and altars where the services could be held, and which would be dedicated to a particular saint whose statue or image would feature prominently in the building or at the altar. In addition many parish churches installed side altars, or chapels, also dedicated to various saints. Often associated with these chapels and altars would be organizations called confraternities. These organizations were set up not only so that they could pay a priest to pray for the members, but also to act as charitable organizations, looking after their own members who were sick or poor, or elderly, even at times distributing gifts to the deserving poor.

The Reformation came rather later to Guernsey than it did to England. The Islands were under the jurisdiction of the Catholic bishops of Coutances who in the person of Bishop Etienne Martel de Basqueville (bishop from 1557 to 1560) issued their last recorded act of jurisdiction in 1557, whereas Henry VIII's break with the Pope had occurred in 1534. In

1568 the new Dean of Guernsey, Dean After, refused to swear obedience to the Bishop of Coutances. This then led Queen Elizabeth I to order the Channel Islands to be subject to the Bishop of Winchester.

With the coming of the Reformation of this Island, only one of two of the Rectors refused to submit to the new type of religion. They were expelled from Guernsey.

For a time Catholic services were held in secret, and if anyone was caught, they would be punished quite severely. Indeed, on one occasion one member of the Castel Parish was whipped through the Town for having attended a secret Catholic service.

Church of St Marie du Castel.

As time went by, Guernsey received Protestant refugees from France which had remained Catholic. With the outbreak of the French Wars of Religion in 1562 these numbers increased so that there were men capable and anxious to preach to Guernsey people in French, a language somewhat familiar to the Islanders who spoke Norman-French.

Unfortunately, however, these preachers were followers of John Calvin, a French religious reformer of a very strict type. They introduced the Calvinist system to the Island. Supported by the courts, Calvinism spread throughout Guernsey and eventually this form of religion became more tyrannical than anything that had preceded it. Thus, the celebration of Saints' days, weddings, funerals, engagements, etc., were either banned or strictly controlled.

Under the Calvinists everyone had to go to Church twice every Sunday, or supply the Parish Minister with the reason for absence. In addition the Church Assemblies met regularly and heard reports of lapses in their very strict rules of behaviour on the part of members of the congregation. Infringement of these rules was dealt with severely.

The ordinary daily life of the people was seriously disrupted, thus horse-riding on a Sunday was forbidden whilst the singing of what were considered unsuitable songs was not allowed nor were gambling and dancing permitted.

When people were referred to the Court, the sentences included flogging, the Stocks, imprisonment in the lowest of the Castle Cornet dungeons (to be fed on bread and water), the town Cage and corporal punishment.

Another aspect of Calvinism was its extreme hatred of witchcraft. Between 1550 and 1650 at least 100 persons were accused of witchcraft in Guernsey. Torture was used to force people to admit that they practiced witchcraft, and when they confessed, punishments such as flogging, banishment, hanging, burning at the stake, and strangulation were handed out.

Education was very much under the control of the Calvinist system. School teachers were first nominated and examined by the Parish Ministers as to their way of life, etc. When appointed they had to take the children to church so that they could listen to a sermon and hear the church rules in order that they might answer questions from the Minister. School teachers were also expected to help and recommend any promising pupils who could eventually obtain help from the States to continue their education at the Universities of Saumur in France, or Cambridge in England. The object of course was to produce men to fill vacancies for ministers in the Island Churches.

The church buildings too underwent tremendous changes, including the obliteration of any ancient paintings on the walls, once used to instruct the congregation. Statues and images were smashed or removed and the walls whitewashed. Stone altars were removed and replaced by wooden tables and stone fonts were replaced by glass bowls. Memorial plaques and chancel screens were taken away. Services were stripped of ceremonial actions, such as the use of the sign of the cross in baptism. All crosses were broken up, including those on the church roof, in the church itself, and those along the ancient paths leading to the churches.

The first Calvinist Minister appointed to the Castel Parish was Nicholas Effard, who resigned in the same year as he was appointed (1584). He was followed by Jacques Roullees who was also Minister of St Andrew's. There followed a succession of Calvinist Ministers until Charles de la Marche who was appointed in 1655 and resigned in 1662 on the passing of the Act of Uniformity by Charles II, which ordered the use of the Book of the Common Prayer.

The Restoration of the English Monarchy took place in 1660, when after the death of Oliver Cromwell and the resignation as Protector by his son that Charles Stuart, the late King's son, was invited by Parliament to return as King.

King Charles II as he became known made it quite clear that he would not allow Calvinism anywhere in the realm and taking heed of this order in 1662 the Castel Church adopted the Anglican (Church of England) branch of the Christian Church. However, it took very many years before all small remnants of the Calvinist way of worshipping God entirely disappeared from the Anglican Churches of Guernsey.

The Castel School

ALTHOUGH there are no very definite records of the existence of a school at the Castel before 1675, Pierre Le Roy in his well known diary mentions that his son William in 1653 had been appointed Verger and Clerk at the Castel, having been Schoolmaster for a long time before this appointment.

In 1675, through the kindness of the widow of James Guille, permission was given for the former Roman Catholic Chapel on the St George Estate to be used as a school.

Little is known concerning the school when it was held in the Chapel although when consulting the note books of John Guille of St George dated 1674-1721 I found the following entry "Paid Maitre Louis Michau 3 sols for teaching my two big children. Paid 9 sols for the schooling of my children for the last three weeks — Paid 4½ sols for the schooling of my three big children for one week and 15 sols for coals as their contribution for the winter".

It is also interesting to find that in 1694 Queen Mary of the William and Mary era gave timber to the parish which was to be used to repair the Church and the School.

Southern end of building once used for Boys and Girls.

The Chapel on St George Estate was closed at the Reformation when another form of worship — very strict Calvanism — was established in the Island. Because at that time the whole Island was French speaking the only suitable Pastors to be found were French Huguenot refugees escaping from Catholic persecution in France. These Pastors and their followers had immense power in the Island and were practically responsible for the appointment and for the instruction given, particularly to religious education. They checked the conduct of teachers and were responsible for the inspection of the children. Indeed as early as 1549 all vestiges of Catholicism had been swept away.

By 1662 after the Restoration of a king in England, King Charles II ordered that the Church of England services should be the form of worship to be used in his domaines but in Guernsey the plain, very strict Calvanist way lingered on partly owing to the difficulty of finding French speaking Church of England Ministers.

In October 1755 the Rector and Church wardens accepted the gift of an annual sum of money from Dame Marie de Saumarez with which to build and maintain a school, a site having been donated by Mons Elizee le Marchant which consisted of a plot already partly occupied by the ruins of a windmill formally used to grind corn.

The money available proved inadequate so that the church and parishioners had to help. Many people promised annual payments (known as rentes) from their farms and some gave subscriptions. A headmaster was appointed but the school remained small until compulsory school attendance was introduced.

The School was completed in 1736 — close to the present road leading to St Germain and in 1808 Admiral Sir James (later Lord) de Saumarez promised an annual sum to pay a mistress so that the girls could be separated from the boys and taught reading, sewing and the principles of the Christian Religion.

Then in 1821 the school was again enlarged but being a long narrow building it was difficult to heat and the row of toilets behind the building could be very "smelly".

Up to this point in the history of the School the funds had been provided from Charitable sources but the two large rooms built of Cobo Granite in 1872 were provided by the

Southern side of new building.

Parish and the States. One room was used by the girls and the other by the boys — the old building being destroyed.

Mr James Duquemin was the architect by virtue of being the States Architect and it appears that he received much praise for the way in which the building had been designed, the boys' room being entered by a partition between boys' and girls' rooms. The partition between the rooms consisted of fine rolling doors. When necessary for special occasions the partition could be rolled back to produce what was regarded as one big splendid room.

At the opening the Rev. F. C. Carey conducted a service and Mrs Carey accompanied the hymns on the Harmonium. Addresses were delivered by various well known people and visitors were supplied with luncheon whilst the children from the Castel, Cobo Infant School and Les Eturs Infant School numbering 300 were provided with tea. Lastly the band of the North Militia Regiment played with the permission of their Colonel and helped to make the fete a success.

In 1895 extra classrooms were added, again in Cobo Granite, and the whole building was modernised as separate classrooms were provided.

In 1910 a completely new school was built for the boys — built with the "bluish" granite from the north of the Island whilst a high wall of Cobo Granite separated the boys from the girls.

Nineteen hundred and forty brought a great shock to the Island and the threat of Occupation produced an organised Evacuation. However owing to a misunderstanding concerning the time of departure of a ship a great many Castel children remained in Guernsey and were educated in the Castel School along with children from Colleges and Intermediate Schools whose parents had refused Evacuation. Eventually the most promising children entered the Occupation Intermediate School where they worked very well. From this period Boys and Girls worked together.

The period of the Occupation was grim as eventually the German Forces took over both school buildings and classes were opened in private premises usually in use by the school until the Germans demanded the premises for themselves. In fact one set of desks, chairs etc made 6 journeys across the Parish.

Southern side, built in 1910 to accommodate Boys (only).

Since the liberation the following alterations and additions were carried out. First of all the locks were returned to the doors of classrooms etc and a large shed built by the German forces was put to School use.

Whilst seniors were still educated at the school, horticulture was a serious part of the curriculum and rewarding experiments were carried out.

Thus, experiments were conducted with the soil-less culti-vation of tomatoes and were very successful and tomatoes were also grown normally in steam sterilised soil. The girls grew flowers and helped with the tomatoes. All this was made possible by the generosity of a near-by grower who even allowed the heating of one of the greenhouses.

In addition through the kindness of the late Mr F. Best it was possible to cultivate a patch of untouched land in the now completely empty St Germain Quarry. When this was no longer available a patch on the edge of the playing field was used.

When Les Beaucamps School was opened in 1959 the school lost all the senior pupils so changing it to a Primary School. Some considerable time previously, because of the generosity of the then owner of St George Estate, the school had acquired a Playing Field at a reasonable rent, which it has retained.

One of the greatest boons acquired was a heated swimming pool obtained with considerable assistance from parents and friends. This proved to be a really valuable teaching aid.

With the movement of population into the Parish, numbers

Western side of building showing former Boys' School and three temporary classrooms used when school was overcrowded. Part of the swimming pool can also be seen.

159

rose to 640 which was unprecedented. To cope with this number, 10 extra classrooms, eight around the playground, one at St Matthew's Church Institute and one at the re-opened Eturs Infants School, were brought into use.

This situation hastened the planned major extension and renovation of the buildings. Thus a useless wall, outdoor toilets, etc., were demolished and in their place a new double storey structure was erected joining the two old granite build-ings and providing six new classrooms, toilets and cloakroom facilities. In addition a new Assembly Hall was built as well as an Office, Staff room and kitchen whilst all classrooms were refitted and decorated and a central heating system installed.

Whilst all this work was being carried on, the playing space was reduced to a considerable extent and it was a great relief to the staff when an adjoining field was bought by the Council.

In 1974 the Mare de Carteret School was opened and brought great relief to the Castel School and numbers dropped to 440.

Since this period a number of welcome improvements have been carried out and the number on books has fallen to 363 but is likely to increase in the future.

Guernsey families take refuge in America

GUERNSEY County U.S.A. lies in the eastern half of the State of Ohio, some 25 miles west of the Ohio River. Cambridge, on a tributary river, is the County town and has a population now probably in excess of 18,000. A dozen miles north of Cambridge there is a village called Guernsey but most of the inhabitants appear to have but a hazy idea of the origin of the name of their village and County.

Guernsey County obtained its name from the Guernsey Island emigrants who settled there in the early part of the 19th Century and when Mr F. d'A. Collings visited the area the population of Guernsey County was 42,000 although its area was more than twenty times the size of Guernsey.

The original Guernsey settlers arrived in the year 1806 and appear to have left Guernsey to get away from an atmosphere of economic depression and the threat of enemy action. The pioneering group included twenty eight persons and they were certainly helped by the Sarchet brothers, Thomas (born in 1770) who was the leader and the only one among them fluent in English, John, Nicolas and Peter, all of them with their families. Thus, Anne Bichard (wife of Thomas) looked after their four sons and two daughters. Also in the group was their sister Judith with her husband Daniel Ferbrache.

They left carrying their life savings with them and first of all went to Jersey in a fishing boat where they joined an emigrant ship and nearly lost one of the teenage Sarchet boys. He was in the process of being abducted by the Royal Navy in St Helier and only rescued with considerable difficulty.

One day out and their ship was approached by a French cruiser, causing considerable alarm to the passengers. However the resourceful Captain took out the American Flag and the Frenchman sheared off. They then had to go through a week of calms and eventually arrived in Virginia on June 3rd 1806, after a month at sea.

There they transferred to a smaller vessel for a trip up the Chesapeake Bay to Baltimore, Maryland. According to Mrs

Photograph of Thomas Ferbrache, born in Guernsey 1796 — arrived in Guernsey County, Ohio in 1879.

Sara Amos of Guernsey County there is a quoted memory that the captain comforted himself with too much liquor, so that eventually his passengers mutineered and kept him in chains while John Sarchet took over as Master. Eventually they reached what was regarded as the traditional starting point for overland journeys and here they bought three horse wagons each capable of carrying five tons of goods. Twelve horses were also bought and when these were loaded up they set off westward and commenced a journey which they found to be tough going as there had been exceptionally heavy rains and mud was everywhere. In addition they had to learn new techniques, such as how to drag heavy lumps of timber behind the wagons when on down-slopes to prevent the wagons from over-running the horses.

Nothing in their Guernsey background had prepared them for heat and the insects and animal life of the rugged Appalachian mountains in full summer. Somewhere a child of Peter Sarchet died and was buried in the woods beside the trail. Apparently such pioneer graves are still found today.

Eventually they reached Wheeling (now in West Virginia) which was then the frontier of the civilised world and then they were faced with having to cross the Ohio River by ferry into the largely empty territory beyond. This is where the women were in a rebellious mood and put their feet down. But they were fortunate because on the day they arrived building plots were for sale and they bought plots and erected cabins and later permanent homes.

The few settlers in Cambridge at that time went to see the new arrivals. They found a strange people. The women wore short dresses and gowns, belted around the waist, and large frilled caps. But what was stranger still, they spoke a language that was hard for the settlers to understand. John Sarchet, who could speak some English, explained in a broken way that they were Norman-French folks who had come from the Island of Guernsey to establish homes in America.

Other groups came on later and gradually Guernsey people settled down to their new life. Thus in 1808 Thomas Sarchet opened the first shop in Cambridge which was an adventurous undertaking as he had to journey back to Philadelphia or Baltimore each year to procure merchandise. He also started the first Methodist Church in his house, planted the first apple trees and organised the mining of salt deposits found nearby.

One of the other Sarchet brothers became a carpenter, another a blacksmith, so that it was possible for houses to be built and occupied.

The first white child to be born in the area was delivered of Judith Ferbrache and named Daniel.

In her essays on Guernsey History, Miss Edith Carey informs us of an unexpected addition to the Guernsey County sometime after the first group had established themselves in Ohio. This addition was made by a member of the Ogier family.

The reason for this addition was the presence in Guernsey in the winter of 1799 of two divisions of Russian troops who had been fighting in Holland under Sir Ralph Abercrombie and the Duke of York.

Some had been landing in Jersey but about 6,000 men were quartered at Delancey, partly in existing barracks and partly in wooden huts.

It appears that they were landed in the Channel Islands because the laws of England prevented the importation of Foreign Troops.

The troops were poorly rationed and as might have been expected helped themselves to poultry, vegetables and fruit from the neighbours.

One morning Mr Ogier went out early to shoot wild duck and in coming home with his loaded gun and in the dusk of the early morning he saw a man stealing his apples. He fired at the man's legs and the man went off leaving a track of blood which being followed, led to his corpse being found in a ditch.

Remorseful and frightened Mr Ogier took refuge in the Ville Baudu until the hue and cry appeared to be over and then he slipped over to France and thence to America whence he drifted to Ohio and to what is now Guernsey County.

He made money out there by his diligence and ability and wrote home to his family asking them to come over to him. This they did and reports which I have read indicate that the new family settled down well and prospered.

St Germain Quarry
Golden Gravel as used by the gentry

TO THE west of the parish school, the Route de St Germain runs down towards Vazon. I have known the area since I was a boy and I remember well when 'golden gravel as used by the gentry' was quarried by the employees of the late Ernest Falla, of Le Mount Plaisant. He was the son of Frederick Falla who may have started the present quarry. However, this area appears to have been quarried for a very long time as records make reference to Jean du Fro who worked a quarry in this area in 1639.

The quarry, as used in Mr Falla's day, was considerably smaller than it is at present because under Mr Frederick Best's ownership my father's small adjoining quarry and field were bought and added to the existing area.

Mr Best continued to produce and sell the very popular golden gravel which was to be seen adorning paths all over the island. It would appear to have been obtained by crushing the decaying Cobo granite or Adamellite.

Actually the quarry is the meeting place of several rock types, including Perelle gneiss, which is a hard blue rock hardly distinguishable from the product of the northern quarries. However, having been formed under enormous pressure careful examination will reveal the lines of pressure.

Another rock present is called Cobo Granite and is the youngest rock in the quarry. It was forced to the surface while still malleable — often being forced through existing semi-molten rock, which is now a black, hard and a very heavy rock called dolerite which at one time was used to provide the foundation of new roads.

Eventually Mr Best leased the quarry to a succession of businesses, each following the other. One particular firm was especially progressive crushing golden gravel for sale as well as for inclusion in modules which with the inclusion of peat were sold to growers, the gravel providing drainage.

This same business enterprise also provided the States with huge blocks of stone to be used for coastal defence.

When eventually there were further changes in tenancy, the quarrying came to an end and the quarry was used for other purposes.

A remarkable feature of the quarry is a powerful spring which in ancient times, fed the holy well dedicated to St Germain.

Pool of water at east end of St Germain Quarry before 'dumping' commenced.

The benefit provided by water from this well was recorded as being especially helpful to people suffering from diseases of the legs. My father remembered how in his youth people carrying large milk cans would collect water from the reservoir which my grandfather had built to store water draining from the holy well which, by then, had been rendered difficult to use.

Incidentally, when a student in science, I examined the water and found that it had an extraordinary high mineral content so that it is left to us to decide whether the water really has a medicinal value and whether the sufferers' beliefs were founded on faith or fiction.

At present the overflow from the spring at all seasons enters the drainage system and finds its way to Vazon Bay.

Besides the holy well the Roman Catholic hierarchy established a chapel in the area — now a quarry — and in addition erected a cross and both chapel and cross appear to have been dedicated to St Germain.

Both chapel and cross were situated along the church path leading to the Castel Church and was used by the parishioners of Vazon.

But why St Germanus — well it appears that St Germanus was born in Auxerre (c. 418 to 448) and that he was a member of one of the noblest families in Gaul which then like the remainder of the Roman Empire was Christian. He is said to have had an extremely good education and so rose to high office enjoying life to the full, hunting being his favourite sport. It is reported that he hung the favourite trophies of the chase, according to old custom, on a certain tree which because of its pagan association angered the Bishop of Auxerre who finding his pleadings useless eventually cut the tree down and burnt it along with all the trophies.

The story then continues that Germanus, extremely angry, set off to kill the Bishop but after an encounter between them in the Church, Germanus is said to have come out a changed man, giving himself up to good works, giving away his great wealth to the poor and needy. Eventually, when the Bishop died, the former great nobleman became the Bishop of Auxerre.

He was sent by the Pope to Britain in 429 to help the British Christians. He was not only a great teacher but was also a competent soldier and he helped to organise the resistance of the Britons against the invading Saxons.

Auxerre was a great teaching centre and St Patrick studied there before evangelising Ireland. St Illud was a pupil of St Germanus and developed the monasteries of South Wales whence came St Sampson, etc. St Germanus and his pupils were thus important figures in the development of the Christian Church after the collapse of Roman administration in Britain and Brittany and it is not surprising that the early Christian missionaries to this Island, like St Sampson, chose to honour St Germanus when they Christianised this site of pagan worship lying to the north of the Hougue which was then known as Le Tertre de Raulf d'Albec and where we now have the St Germain Quarry.

Finally some while ago I came across some interesting comments regarding the St Germain area. The note was

Appearance of St Germain Quarry west end — before 'dumping' commenced.

dated 1552 and mentioned the pretty path leading to the fisherman's Chapel, which had apparently been widened. The spring was also mentioned in connection with its medical properties. Thus it was recorded that 'the sacred fire' could be cured by water from the spring. Apparently this disease caused fever and produced a deep red colour of the skin. It is described as a local complaint which has also been called 'St Anthony's Fire' and erysipelas.

Since writing the above great changes have occurred in respect of the quarry as the States of Guernsey have found it absolutely essential to start filling the quarry with builders' rubbish and similar material.

They have done this in close co-operation with the Parish Constables and Douzaine, the latter laying down certain conditions which include excluding all toxic material from being deposited in the quarry. They have also forbidden the passage of lorries containing material for the quarry from passing in front of the school during periods when the school is used by scholars.

This last condition has forced the responsible committee to break through the grassy lane to the west of the quarry in order to form a new entrance by piercing through the furze brake so that the new pathway reaches the roadway near La Hougue.

Stories of the little people
told around the Terpi

IN DAYS not so long ago, the winter evenings were spent in very different ways from those today. In my own youth there were no radios or television sets — indeed, no electrical services of any kind were to be found in the average home.

It is true that we had oil lamps and candles which gave enough light to enable the adults to read and play games of many different kinds, while the children amused themselves with toys. It was also the rule to visit relatives, especially during the festive season, there to enjoy a party atmosphere.

Delving back to an earlier age, the custom of visiting one another's homes was a very common way of passing the long winter evenings. The women took their knitting with them and the men hoped that the cider barrel was in good condition and that their pipes would behave.

In this way people shared light and fuel. This was important, as coal was scarce and sometimes hoarded for many years while the 'terpi' in the large open fireplace was kept burning

Illustration of crasset in use, from the Folk Museum.

170

A crasset, photographed at the Folk Museum.

with gorse, 'buzzets' (cakes of dried cow dung), dried peat, waste wood, etc.

At one time in such homes, the light was provided by a 'crasset' which used oil as fuel and provided a small oily flame. The oil used in the 'crasset' continued to be used until the middle of the 19th century.

In the corner was the 'lliatte d'fouille' or 'jonctiere', a flat, wooden structure stuffed with suitable material which eventually developed into a 'green bed'.

Around this a number of women could sit while the men used the only available chairs and the children sat on the floor using large mats of plaited rushes.

This was a time for story-telling and the task would be entrusted to the 'story-teller' of the group who had earned his reputation thanks to his vivid imagination. He might well start by telling a story concerning fairies which he learned from his parents.

However innocuous the beginning, the story might well produce a heated argument concerning the reality of fairies — a strong believer protesting that he knew a man who had actually seen a fairy coming out of the Creux des Fées at Vazon (the Fairies Cave) and so the argument would continue.

However, if we delve even further back we discover that the belief in fairies was international and quite recently I asked an Irishman if any of his compatriots still believed in leprachauns. He assured me that many still believed in the existence of these dainty little folk.

It does seem to me that the existence of fairies and related folk was introduced in order to try to explain phenomena which could not otherwise be explained by logical means.

In certain cases the 'little people' were imagined to exist as creatures with such magical powers that they were able to lift huge stones and build the structures which we call dolmens. Mysterious caves and caverns like the Creux des Fees at Vazon were associated with fairies, about whom a number of stories are told.

Le Creux des Fées is really a double cave — there being

Creux des Fées — Fairies Cave at Vazon.

172

two caves side by side in the eroded portion of the cliff —
and one of the tales about it runs thus:

Once upon a time there lived a girl at Vazon who was
extraordinarily beautiful, and one morning as she was milking
the cows she suddenly saw, coming towards her, a very handsome young man of small stature dressed in green.

The girl was struck by the appearance of this handsome
stranger and when he saw the beautiful girl he could not
help asking her to become his wife and to accompany him to
fairyland.

Some years later the people of Vazon were horrified to see
masses of small, armed men issuing from the Creux des Fées
who maintained that since one of their number had managed
to find such a beautiful girl in Guernsey, they had all come
to capture all the wives and daughters of the island and to
make them their wives.

The Guernseymen defended their womenfolk with vigour
but what chance did they have against supernatural beings?
All were killed except two men of St Andrew's, who hid in
an oven.

The fairymen took the place of the island's menfolk and
decided to stay in the island until they were forced to return
to their own land.

The strangers cultivated the soil and looked after the cattle
just as the menfolk had done, but eventually they were
forced by their own rules to leave the island and their wives
and families.

However, their children grew up to be short in stature and
only the children of the men who had hidden in the oven
were tall.

This was, of course, a fairy story which fantasised the
story of Owen of Wales, who attacked the island in 1372 and
landed his troops in Vazon Bay. He caused much slaughter
but failed to capture the island.

Secondly, the fairy story drew attention to the fact that for
a long time the island had very many short men and fewer
tall ones.

The Creux des Fées is made up of two caves — a large
one penetrating deeply into the land and a small one with a
narrow entrance and passage which penetrates inwards until
it reaches a chamber with a 'table' composed of a block of
granite.

Inlet from sea to Le Creux des Fées.

As a boy I ventured into the very narrow passage of this cave and found the huge flat block of stone. But I was somewhat disappointed not to find it covered with golden goblets and plates that my father had told me would be ready for the fairies' next meal.

The next occasion that I found the opening to the narrow cave free of pebbles was when I took a party of young children from the Castel School to see the caves.

They were armed with torches and after a difficult climb down to the floor of the caves, a number of them suddenly disappeared into the small cave and around the sharp bend in the passage.

During the time that the children were out of sight I was really concerned as to what I should do if one became stuck in the very narrow passage. I felt that the rising tide would give little time for any rescue to be organised.

However, my worries were soon over and the children returned saying that they had seen the fairy table but like me they were disappointed by the absence of the lovely golden tableware belonging to the fairies.

The children also explored the large cave but found that although wider and longer than the other one, it also came to an abrupt end (despite old stories that a passage penetrated inland to end in the neighbourhood of a church on the western side of the island).

174

Some have suggested that the large cave would have been very useful to smugglers but commonsense leads to the conclusion that the regular use of this cave by smugglers is extremely doubtful.

As a final note I would like to emphasise that the approach to the Creux des Fées is not suitable for young children to attempt without assistance. It can be rather dangerous for those unaccustomed to rock-climbing.

Cobo Soup Kitchen

THE Cobo Soup Kitchen was an independent organisation made up of persons who during the Occupation were conscious of the need to maintain the health and stamina of the younger generation and the work of this group was particularly appreciated towards the end of the Occupation, when islanders were without bread.

At this time the children who attended the kitchen had had nothing substantial to eat since the previous day and competed with each other on the number of bowlfuls that they could consume!

The president of the committee which was formed to administer the kitchen was Harry Ozanne, of Lilyvale, who made himself responsible for the organisation of the enterprise.

My own role was to help to find some of the food and money required. However, there is no doubt at all that the real heroines in this successful undertaking were the late Miss Doris Le Tissier and Miss D. Young, who were responsible for the preparation and provision of the soup. They were assisted by a band of willing helpers who also helped to distribute bowls of soup among the children.

Another great helper was Jack Andre, who acted as the treasurer of the Soup Kitchen, and worked very hard in many other ways, especially as far as the provision of food supplies was concerned.

My father, who was pictured with a damaged arm, also worked extremely hard behind the scenes peeling potatoes and transporting goods with a horse and van.

Unfortunately, the only potatoes available to the Soup Kitchen were 'pig potatoes' — the small ones which were so difficult to peel. However, John Upham very kindly repaired and restored a potato peeler which had been considered to be damaged beyond repair. This was used by my father, who appointed himself as potato peeler and general carrier for the remainder of the Occupation.

Surprisingly we did not find ourselves short of money as we received financial help from the *Star* newspaper's Help

'Copper' as used at Soup Kitchen.

'Coppers' built and used when the gas supplies were no longer available.

the Children Appeal, from Mr J. B. Tetley (the then owner of St George Estate) and from the Education Council.

The need for help for the children became very real and I remember the day when I found out that of the 44 children having lunch at school, 24 had only one slice of bread, 14 had but half a slice and six had no bread at all!

It was then decided that the Soup Kitchen would function twice a week.

But as time went on, and particularly while Guernsey was without bread, the number of soup days was increased to five — and during this period no fewer than 6,142 meals were served.

At first the soup was prepared using gas cookers but in January 1945, when the island was practically cut off from all gas supplies, the organisers had to turn to the old-fashioned coppers which had long been used for boiling water, etc. These were solidly installed on a framework of bricks obtained by demolishing an old greenhouse chimney.

But the use of coppers meant that there was another burden placed upon those responsible for the cooking, as wood had to be found to light the fires and cook the soup.

The soup supplied at Cobo was of good quality as may be

A Real Heroine — Miss Doris Le Tissier.

179

seen from the following list of vegetables which was considered sufficient to provide soup for 90 children: potatoes—90lb. per week; carrots—90lb. per week; parsnips— 30lb. per week; beans—12lb. per week; cauliflowers—36lb. per week; onions— 18lb. per week.

Bones were obtained from butchers who quite often managed to exercise generosity regarding the amount of meat remaining on them.

The number of children served with meals during the period mid-1943 to Liberation was 21,504, a figure of which the workers at Cobo had every reason to be proud. Actually, during the period of extreme food scarcity on 20 February 1945, 140 meals were supplied.

I cannot forget certain events which took place just before the first breadless period. These were set into motion when I received a phone call from Miss Le Tissier to inform me that stocks of food were extremely low and that she had prayed and hoped, but unless something happened to change the situation, the Soup Kitchen would have to close down.

I cycled to Town and approached the offices of those responsible for organising the food supply for the island but was not successful in obtaining any help, or promise of help, as the vegetables available to the public were strictly rationed.

I came home quite depressed but as I entered the house the telephone rang. When I answered a voice speaking in Guernsey-French offered me some vegetables for the Soup Kitchen.

Of course, I was delighted but said that I doubted the ability of the speaker to supply anything like the quantity required. I was then asked to give an idea of the amount required.

I replied, 'Ten tons,' and to my astonishment the speaker asked whether I was sure that was enough, to which I replied that he could make it 14 tons if he wished!

It was then that the identity of the speaker revealed himself as Mr, later Jurat, T. Le M. Allez, who was one of the administrators responsible for island food supplies.

I discovered that it was food designated for German use that he was offering but my father offered to collect it from fields at St Saviour's, controlled by Mr C. H. Moullin, of Doulieu, St Saviour's.

My father used to tell how he often went into a field and

180

Committee and helpers of the Cobo Soup Kitchen, September 1943 to May 1945.

loaded carrots while the Germans were busy doing the same thing at the other end of the field. No one ever questioned him and secrecy was maintained at home where the roots were stored in a large loft above my father's bedroom.

A hook in the outside wall enabled the goods to be pulled up or lowered down.

Miss Le Tissier was delighted and regarded the whole development as an answer to her prayers.

Jurat Allez took a considerable risk in helping our children and without the assistance of such an individual we would not have been able to carry on the very valuable work of the Cobo Soup Kitchen.

The Fate of Our Old Batteries

THE following comprises an official list of the Fortifications given by the States of Guernsey to Her Majesty Queen Victoria. This gift was no doubt appreciated in 1850 when relationships with France and England were not at their best. These strained relations caused by the extensive defence installations being constructed at Cherbourg also involving a great naval harbour with several forts to protect it.

The following long list was eventually included in a comprehensive document authorised by the States of Guernsey when the gift was approved and another prepared when the forts, batteries, magazines, etc., were handed over to the care of the officials of the Crown who became entirely responsible for the defence of the Island.

No   1. Salerie Batterie.
      2. Mont Arrivé Batterie.
      3. Mare Pirouin Battery.
  * 4. Hougue a La Pere Battery and Magazine.
  * 5. Belle Grève Battery and Magazine.
  * 6. Kempt Battery.
      7. Delancey Battery.
      8. Esperon or Spur Battery.
      9. Mont Crevet Watch House.
   10. Houmet Benest Battery.
   11. Noirmont Point Battery.
   12. Beaucette Battery and Magazine.
   13. Fort Le Marchand or Fort de l'Angle and Magazine.
   14. Nid de l'Herbe or Right Battery and Magazine.
   15. Centre Battery and Magazine.
 *16. Half Moon Battery.
   17. Estequet or Left Battery L'Ancresse Bay.
   18. Platon Battery.
   19. Mont Chouet, alias Mont Cuette Batteries and Magazine.
   20. Picquerie Battery.
   21. Rousse Battery and Magazine.
   22. Portinfer Battery.

23. Grandes Rocques Battery and Magazine.
*24. Salines Battery.
*25. Cobo North Battery.
*26. Cobo South Battery.
27. Cobo Magazine.
28. Roque du Guet Battery and Watch House.
29. Burton Battery and Magazine.
30. Houmet Battery and Magazine.

"Martello Tower" at Houmet, Vazon.

31. Vazon or Right Battery Vazon Bay Magazine.
*32. Vazon Centre or Grande Mare Battery and Magazine.
*33. Blondel Battery.
*34. Left Vazon or Moullin Battery.
35. Le Crocq Point Battery and Magazine.
*36. Richmond Battery and Magazine.
*37. Perelle Battery and Magazine.
38. Mont Chnichon or Druid's Altar Battery and Magazine.
*39. Catioroc Watch House.
40. Tuzel Battery or Le Ree Point Battery and Magazine.
*41. Rocquaine Battery or Brock Fort and Magazine.
42. Fort Pezerie and Magazine.
43. Pleinmont or Petites Portes Battery.
44. Narrow Point or Grandes Portes Battery.
45. Pleinmont Watch House.
46. Mont Herault Watch House.
*47. Les Tielles Watch House and Battery.

*48. Prevote Watch House (in ruins).
49. Sommeilleuse Magazine.
50. Bouferesse or St Clair's Battery and Magazine.
51. Icart Battery.
52. Cannuet or Saint's Bay Right Battery and Magazine.
53. Saint's Bay — Left Battery.
54. Bon Port or Moulin Huet Right Battery.
55. Moulin Huet Battery and Watch House.
56. La Moie or Tas de Pois d'Ament Battery.
57. Jerbourg Magazine.
58. Mont au Nord Battery or Jerbourg Battery.
59. Cumberland or Bec du Nez Battery and Magazine.
60. Magazine South of Fermain Bay.
61. Fermain Battery South or Right Battery, Fermain Bay.
62. Centre Battery or Fermain Battery and Magazine North.
63. Becquet Platform centre.
64. Becquet Lower Platform.
65. Becquet Upper Battery Magazine and Watch House.
*Now disappeared.

This list gives us some idea of the forts, magazines and batteries which in 1850 were considered to be in such a condition as to be worthy of inclusion in this important list

Showing additions made to fortifications at Vazon. At present only "Martello" section remains.

of fortifications which could easily be adapted to take a place in defending the Island of Guernsey should it be attacked by France.

These fortifications have now disappeared whilst others may have been adapted to more mundane purposes.

Fort Le Crocq — destroyed by the German Forces as it interfered with defensive and offensive needs.

A list of those which have completely disappeared includes the following:—

Hougue a La Pere Battery and Magazine.
Belle Grève Battery and Magazine.
Kempt Battery — a paved platform for one gun fronting the beach.
Fort Souscription — behind Salerie Corner.
Salerie Battery.
Salines Battery — south of Grandes Rocques.
Cobo North.
Cobo South.
Half Moon Battery at L'Ancresse.
Grande Mare Battery.
Blondel Battery — bordering Vazon Bay.
Richmond Battery — West of Richmond Barracks.
Perelle Battery — Fronting Perelle Bay.
Les Tielles — Watch House and Battery.

Prevote Watch House (in ruins).
Brock Fort and Magazine — near the centre of Rocquaine Bay.

There is no doubt that the active state of most of the fortifications, etc., was in no small measure due to the vigour with which at an earlier date Sir John Doyle had committed himself to improving the fortifications of the Island. This did not mean that every single Guernsey fortification had been considered worthy of Sir John's attention and indeed if the names on the list are considered, the omissions which include the coastal towers will become obvious, especially as there are remains of fortifications around the Island which have not yet been fully examined. Of course we now have some which were introduced, altered or improved at some time by the British Forces or eventually by the German Forces.

Finally there is little doubt that some of the fortifications on the list have now disappeared or are difficult to find.

Problems of a Couple in the Autumn of their Lives

THE orphans, the poor, the afflicted and the aged have presented problems practically since mankind first appeared on the earth. Various solutions have been adopted, the usual one being that the unfortunates should be housed and cared for by the younger generation but this solution has not always been very successful in our own civilisation.

Thus misery and want could also exist in cases where no children or near relatives were available to take care of the old, or where serious quarrels had split a family group.

In Guernsey during the Roman Catholic period the Church organised help and relief, particularly through Friaries or brotherhoods which worked very much like the Sick Benefit Clubs that exist at the present time, but all these religious brotherhoods were dissolved with the Reformation and a considerable period elapsed before really sound new facilities were made available for the care of life's truly unfortunate persons.

Recently, on glancing through some old documents I came across a case where a couple who for some reason quite unknown appear to have found themselves unable to run their farm and appear to have thrown themselves at the mercy of a man and his wife, who bore different names to theirs and who could well have been their own employees.

This action constituted a "delaissie" a practice which in certain cases may have worked well but in too many cases proved disastrous. This was particularly true in cases where the whole property was given away to a comparative stranger in return for care and shelter. In such cases the poor individuals concerned could be ignored and sorely neglected. What happened to this particular couple involved in this "delaissie" cannot be traced and the records of burials at the Castel Church have been consulted without result so that it would appear that the couple left the parish or may indeed have left the Island.

Le Carrefour.

The document which I read recorded that on the 12th of June, 1725, in the reign of George I, a Court assembly heard the details of this "delaissie". This court session was presided over by Helier Bonamy esquire, Judge Delegate, whilst George Fiott and Josué Le Marchant were the Jurats. This unusual document was presumably made in order to establish legality to the details of the 'delaissie".

In this document it is recorded that Charles Le Jersiez, son of Pierre of the Castel Parish and Marie Richard his wife, relinquished their rights of ownership in the entire farmstead then known as "Le Carrefour", passing the ownership on to Etienne Breton son of Eliazar but with certain conditions.

These were that Breton would pay annually the 13 quarters of wheat rente that were due on the property. This payment was due to Jacques Quertier the former owner of the farm and Charles Le Jersiez and his wife promised that if this was done they in their turn would transfer the whole farm to the Bretons, free from any other similar payments except Chefrente and other Seignorial rights.

Strangely enough one of these Seignorial demands involved the provision of a Vavasseur (similar to a Jurat) to the Court of Fief de Saumarez according to the obligation attached to the holder of Le Courtil du Bordage to provide a Bordier to act on behalf of the Fief de Saumarez. Such Bordiers were at that time important officials in the conduct of certain fiefs.

188

The more mundane conditions laid down by the Le Jersiez's was that neither Etienne Breton nor his heirs should dig out or carry away any stones from the land and that during the remainder of their life-time the Le Jerseiz couple would have the right of using a bedroom, the right to store fuel in the attic and the right to house a cow, with hay to feed it, in one of the stables, as well as a pig in the sty — all without payment. In addition Le Jersiez and his wife demanded a "Tiercon" (ancient measure) of cider each year and the right to cultivate vegetables in the garden for their own use.

Finally the Bretons were told that they would have the privilege of being able to let their animals graze in "La Cloture du Houmet" during the winter when grazing was scarce but only according to the share which had formerly belonged to Jacques Quertier.

The original deed was dated 1725 and a second document appeared in 1733 recording a court hearing before Josué Le Marchant Esq. Bailiff and Thomas Fiott and Pierre Carey, Jurats. This document indicated that the ageing Charles Le Jersiez and wife had resolved to leave, give up, and totally abandon all their remaining rights in Le Carrefour Farm to Etienne Breton. From this it would appear that the Le Jersiez couple, presumably now elderly, were either throwing themselves completely at the mercy of the Bretons or else they were planning to live with someone else — possibly relatives. In any case they appeared satisfied with the action to be taken.

Something may have gone very wrong, because 45 years afterwards in 1778 a third Court presided over by Bailiff William Le Marchant and Jurats Nicolas Reserson and Jean Carey, studied the two documents possibly because it became necessary to check the legality of the procedure. The need for this review could well have been initiated by the discontent of individuals who without these documents could have been heirs of the valuable property involved. It would appear that the result of this investigation was a decision that all the actions taken had been quite legal in view of the first two Court cases. However it does appear that the "delaissie" was not entirely successful although one must admit that the full facts are not known.

In my youth this farm was still completely intact, the farm-house having panelled interior partitions whilst the front wall was built of beautifully dressed granite which at some time had no doubt replaced the original rough frontage.

Unfortunately as the years went by repairs were neglected so that eventually it was partly demolished and re-built and renamed to become "Le Bourg". The outbuildings were also transformed into dwellings and the entire holding, fields etc was fragmented, bringing to a sad end one of Guernsey's traditional farms.

Now completely renovated, the "Carrefour" has been changed from a farmhouse into a high class residence which until recently was the home of Lady Ann Wellesley and Lady Ann Rhys, members of the Wellington family reputed to own some valuable "Waterloo" relics. It may now have been given a new name of "Le Bourg" but to me it will always be "Le Carrefour" which of course refers to the place where four roads meet — in this case a most appropriate name.

The improved residence is now owned and occupied by Mr. and Mrs. Mitchell who appear to be looking after "Le Bourg" very well indeed.

Le Carrefour transformed into "Le Bourg".

National Trust Property
at Talbot Valley
Talbot Valley tranquillity

I FEEL sure that people will be surprised to find that the National Trust of Guernsey was founded some thirty years ago, possibly acting with a less resolute approach than at present.

At first the object of the National Trust was to hold deserving property as real estate and in perpetuity for the people of Guernsey.

A surprising number of Guernsey's important residents have served on the main controlling committee or on sub-committees of the Trust.

In 1959 the Guernsey Evening Press produced an article extolling the beauty of the Talbot Valley and questioning whether the area could be recognised as a National Park.

There is no doubt at all that the "Press" article was correct in praising the valley as an area of outstanding natural beauty which needed to be protected against indiscriminate building.

Certainly the Island Development Committee strived to carry out this objective and in 1972 the National Trust were particularly fortunate to receive the gift of two plots on one of the most suitable viewing points of the whole valley. This gift was made by Mr Gordon Mont-Ford Chandler to whom the Trust will always be most grateful.

A member of the Trust Mr Ron Short proved to be most anxious to develop the Talbot Valley area in such a way as to enable people to enjoy not only the beauty of the trees, plants and flowers of the area itself but also of the Valley below.

In fact his idea was to try to construct an elevated walk which not only would serve the area already acquired but proceed at a desirable height for a considerable distance towards King's Mills starting at La Ruette de la Torte.

Unfortunately Ron Short died before his dream had been

Castel School children planting trees at the "Ron Short Walk".

put into practice and the responsibility of looking after the area was placed on Mr Roger Bichard and he asked me to interview Mr Thomas Le Pelley of Les Videcins who owned the first field from which a path could be started.

Mr Le Pelley was extremely helpful and generous to the Trust giving a very wide strip of land to form the beginning of the long path which was eventually called the "Ron Short Walk" in memory of the man who had done so much for the National Trust of Guernsey.

Special thanks were also passed on to the Board of Administration which had provided us with the suitable stone-work to use on the construction of the steps at the bottom of La Ruette de la Torte.

Castel School children planting trees on the National Trust land at Talbot Valley.

Responding to the advice coming from so many directions, trees were planted on various places on the property. In fact for a number of years by co-operation of the Education Authorities, the I.D.C. and "The Men of the Trees" groups of school children planted trees in various places on the property, now generally referred to simply as the "Ron Short Walk" although in fact the area in use has been increased by the provision of three paths leading to the road below.

Most of the trees have now reached a considerable size

especially the conifers kindly presented by Mr Short's widow and by Mr P. S. Mansell of The Grange Lodge Hotel. However the pride of the property are beautiful Silver Birch trees planted by children and cared for by Lord Churston the then President of the "Men of the Trees".

View of Talbot Valley from National Trust Property.

Standing high above everything else is an enormous and beautiful Pine tree which was acquired when the land came into the possession of the Trust.

Some Silver Birch trees were planted by ladies of the Women's Institute of Guernsey in order to commemorate the 25th year of our Queen's Accession but they have shown only moderate growth as unfortunately the spot where they were planted was rather too dry for maximum growth.

The facilities offered by this National Trust Property have been considerably increased since the days of Ron Short and Roger Bichard. Two paths have been made, one of which connects the highest point in the area to the quarry which has a reasonable area where car parking is available. The other path joins the summit with a small little known enclosure. Presentation seats have been placed at suitable places where people can relax and admire the beautiful green valley.

These developments were carried out when Mr Hugh Sarre and then Mr John Tostevin presided over the Land Committee.

It is a property which seasonably produces lovely wild flowers which include:

WILD FLOWERS

Alexanders	Foxglove	Ox-eye Daisy
Bluebells	Freesia	Pellitory
Butchers Broom	Fumitory	Pennywort
Buttercups	Gladdon	Periwinkle
Changing	Goosegrass	Plantain
Forget-me-not	Gorse	Red Campion
Charlock	Guernsey Star	Scarlet Pimpernel
Common Cat's ear	of Bethlehem	Sea Campion
Common Field	Hairy Bitter-cress	Smooth Sawthistle
Speedwell	Heath Groundsel	Star of Bethlehem
Common Sorrel	Hedge Bedstraw	Sticky Mouse-ear
Crow Garlia	Herb Robert	Stinking Onions
Cut-leaved	Hogweed	Thale Cress
Dead-nettle	Honeysuckle	Vetch
Dove's foot	Lesser Celandine	Wall Pennywort
Crane's bill	Lords and Ladies	Wood Sage

FERNS

Bracken	Lanceolate
Black Spleenwort	Spleenwort
Harts Tongue	Polypody

and horticultural escapes such as Red Flowered Gladioli, Spring Snowflakes and Daffodils. Adding to the beauty of the area we also have several species of coniferous and deciduous trees.

A mention should also be made of the ferns that help to provide a desirable green colour at points all over the property especially in the early part of the year when the "Ron Short Walk" certainly provides a worthwhile inspection.

Finally all the visitors should spend a little time looking over at the beautiful Talbot Valley which evidently so impressed the "Press" so many years ago.

195

A place for marvelling at Cobo sunsets

APART from the beach, Le Guet is the main attraction to visitors to Cobo, yet there is also much of interest in the district itself. The striking orange and reddish granite, for example, which has given a beautiful colour to the rocks and reefs.

A little while ago, on a summer evening, I chatted to a man well in his nineties who confessed that he loved to view the colour that the setting sun gave to the rocks and he meant to stay at Cobo until the last rays of the setting sun had disappeared. After that, believe it or not, he drove his car back to his Torteval home.

Quarries extracting this stone have been in existence for hundreds of years and Cobo granite has beautified hundreds of homes throughout the islands, besides being used to erect imposing public buildings.

When walking in the district it is possible to gaze at the remains of at least four disused quarries. One facing the sea is of particular interest. At the back is a very tall mass of granite which Lord de Saumarez called 'The Chimney' and when he became the owner of the whole of the Guet he refused to allow this rock to be smashed and it can still be seen just below the Watch House.

As for the Guet property, I remember it covered with clumps of gorse, fern, brambles and hawthorn. Whole areas of coarse grass between exposures of rock provided grazing for my uncle's non-milking stock. It was a typical 'lande' and in time the name was given to the whole district.

In 1732 applications for enclosing the "Lande du Guet" were made. At that time most of the land surrounding the Guet appears to have belonged to two individuals and each was activated by the current enthusiasm for the enclosure of property and, after having received the permission from the Douzaine, on condition that there would be a complete lack of opposition from the neighbours.

The permission dated 31 March 1732 enabled a start to be made on the building of the necessary walls. Eventually a wall was made enclosing the property and separating it from the public road, except where the wall reached the top of Albecq Hill, where stood a very prominent rock which by the order of the Douzaine had to be excluded from the enclosure.

This rock was called Le Rocher au Veau or Calf Rock, and on this triangle an infants' school was built to save the Cobo and Vazon children having to walk a long way to the Castel School. A similar school was built at Les Eturs to cater for the children of that end of the parish, but both schools are now closed.

The Guet without trees but Cobo Hotel can be seen and the Guet Observation Post is very prominent.

Les Eturs was reopened for a short time during the Occupation and again for a few years from 1964 when the Castel School was inundated with children and nine extra classrooms had to be found.

The fate of the Albecq School was very different as it was closed at a much earlier date and sold to a private individual. Finally, during the Occupation, the German Forces demolished it completely for some unknown reason. After the war a private house was built on the spot.

Most, if not all such infant schools built on various parts of the island were supported by religious bodies, and affiliated to Churches and such associations as the Society for the Promotion of Christian Knowledge.

To return to the enclosure, it is interesting that permission

197

to enclose would appear to have included the making of a new road, running from what is now the present Cobo Institute to what was the back of the old Cobo Hotel (which, like the old Cobo Institute, was destroyed by the German Forces).

The road, now disused, was to be clearly marked by stone walls and careful measurements at a selected spot showed that the footpath 'for the convenience of the public' was 4ft in width, while the road was 6ft across. In addition, the depth of the road was some 4ft below the general level.

One stipulation in the permission to enclose has not been maintained and as the property is now in the hands of the States, they could be expected to honour it. This stipulation was that the road was to be kept in good repair.

What puzzles me is why these two men went to the trouble and expense of erecting all these walls. Was it because of the pride of ownership or to prevent the public from regarding the Guet property as common land?

Of course, in those days places like the Guet provided fuel for the baker's ovens — a practice which was not without profit for the property owners concerned. Indeed this factor may have influenced the decision to erect these walls.

At least two other enclosures of interest were made which preserved the right of people to dry seaweed along the sea-shore. One individual concerned was Jean Girard, who in

Detail from an old photograph taken before the war. Note that the coast road follows the sea wall — nowadays it runs very close to the powder magazine.

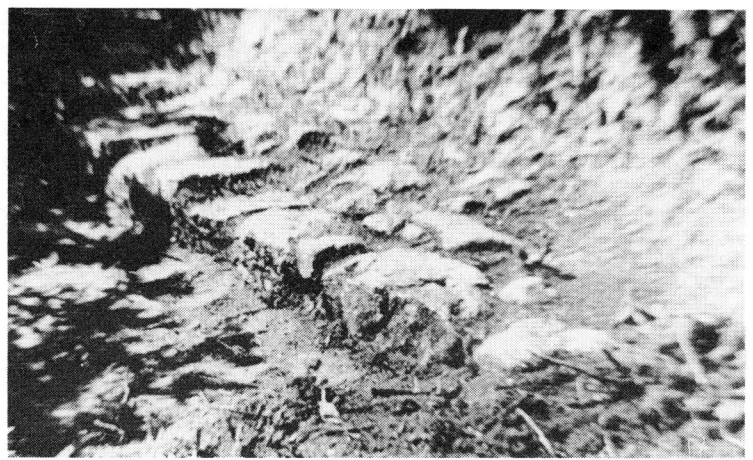

Footpath constructed through Guet property in 1782. Roadway was 6ft in width and footpath 4ft.

1738, was allowed to enclose land near La Banque d'Estrainger, at the foot of the Guet.

With the permission there was a stipulation that he had to leave a gateway sufficiently wide to allow carts to use it without difficulty at all times so that the inhabitants could continue to avail themselves of the area to dry their seaweed, etc.

When a road was first made along this part of the coast, it was constructed close to the then new coast wall but the Germans deviated the coast road, not only to build bunkers, but also to bring their railway from the district of Cobo Farm.

This deviation made it necessary for steps to be built to replace the rather steep slope which had previously provided a means of carrying on the quarrying in the Guet close to the house called Sous La Lande.

I have not mentioned the Guet building because it has been very well covered elsewhere, but I must mention the ruins of a house close to the road near Cobo Institute. It may have been quite a fine house, because some time ago I saw an attractive arch which had been taken away from here and used on another property.

When considering a simple area like the Guet it is amazing how much of interest can be recorded. Fine, finished, flint tools of ancient man were found in the Guet by some Castel School children. These discoveries included a really fine knife with a carefully made saw-like edge.

Realising my ignorance of the way to organise a 'dig', I stopped the children's efforts and although I have mentioned the discovery to a number of archaeologists I have not yet had the satisfaction of seeing a 'dig' carried out at Le Guet.

The sale of the whole of the Guet to the then Lord de Saumarez at the time he was extending his estate, brought great changes to the property.

During the period of his ownership quite extensive quarrying was carried on so that he was able to use the beautiful pink Cobo granite in his building operations. Besides this he allowed some granite to be used for the building of important public amenities.

As far as the land itself is concerned Lord de Saumarez decided to use the Guet to carry out a formidable, carefully planned experiment to find out which pine trees were the most suitable for Guernsey. In this enterprise he was assisted by Major R. G. Davies and Mr Lloyd de Putron.

The Guet was planted in blocks of pine trees obtained from many parts of the world. Now would be the time to assess the success of the experiment, but unfortunately large fires before the war, drought and damage done by the Occupation Forces have made accurate comparison impossible.

Disused quarry at base of Watch-house. Note mass of Cobo granite at back of quarry. This Lord de Saumarez called 'The Chimney' and he refused to allow anyone to quarry it.

Christmas Festivities during the Occupation

AS the festival of Christmas approaches I cannot but remember the ways in which the Castel and no doubt other schools celebrated the first Occupation Christmas. As far as I was concerned the first development was the organising of two parties for the two hundred children at the Castel School.

One party was organised for the senior children and another for the younger ones and they all received gifts. In the case of the senior children they received gifts allotted to them by the organisers of the "Star" newspaper's special children's fund, whilst the younger ones received gifts provided by the School Committee which included welcome bags of sweets.

Father Christmas (the late Mr Stan Keyho) attended the two parties at the school and music and songs brightened up the occasion.

The Christmas period of 1941/42 brought much help from friends who assisted in running parties at the Delisles Sunday School. Toys presented were obtained from an appeal conducted by Mr Winterflood, the Secretary of the Education Council. In addition Mr J. E. B. Tetley, the owner of St George Estate, presented all the children with gifts of money. He also provided a Christmas tree and decorations which he hung up to beautify the hall.

The third Christmas brought with it hungry children and Mr Tetley offered to help to provide the best possible Christmas meal as well as assisting in other ways. He maintained that he had looked after his own children by sending them to England to live with relatives and so he felt that it was his duty to do everything possible for the benefit of the Castel children.

Mr Tetley pointed out that since he was sure that his children would be well entertained at Christmas he felt that he should ensure that the Castel children should have at least one happy day at Christmas.

As a result of our interview a working party was formed

201

CASTEL
NEW YEAR TREAT

January 16th and 17th, 1942.

MENU

Potage Delisle

Cottage Pie au Tertre

Semolina aux Etats de Guernesey

Tartlets André

Cordials a la Paix

which consisted of Mr Tetley, the late Mr John Andre, his mother, my wife and myself.

All our meetings were conducted in a cottage situated in the grounds of St George where Mr Tetley had been sent whilst the main house was occupied by members of the German army.

All who could do so were asked to co-operate and I well remember Mr Andre and myself setting out in snow, seated in a van drawn by my ever willing horse, our objective being to collect gifts for the children's Christmas party.

I well remember the outstanding generosity of parishioners as we collected fowls, vegetables, wheat (to be ground into flour) and in addition small quantities of groceries and even rabbits, some of the latter having been snared in Herm by some of the parents.

Mr Tetley provided thick 'stock' which we found out afterwards had been produced from the meat of an animal killed on Mr Tetley's property and whose meat had been boiled in a copper to provide the much appreciated 'stock'. Mr Tetley also provided other valuable items which were welcomed by the cooks.

The main meal was cooked in my father's enormous furze oven which was heated with gorse, by a local expert namely the late Mr Ernest Le Tocq of Les Queritez, Castel.

My father was most anxious that the pans containing the food should be well and truly cooked and he kept on bothering Ernest who in the end lost his temper and reminded my father in very definite terms that this was not the first time that he had cooked a meal in a Guernsey furze oven.

It had been arranged that the meal and party would be held in the Delisles Sunday School which had been beautifully decorated and fully prepared for the invasion of the children by a number of dedicated helpers.

The transport of the cooked meal had to be faced and the horse and van again came on the scene as the van was transformed into a mobile 'hay box' which was carefully filled. A telephone message was then made to warn the helpers at Delisles that the meal was ready.

Soon we were on the way and my horse took us towards the Delisles at such a pace that my companion almost threatened to jump out.

The main meal reached the table so quickly that it was

really hot and extremely good whilst the 'sweets' which followed were welcomed by the hungry children. This portion of the festivities had been left to the lady helpers and consisted of attractive 'goodies' made from such ingredients as carrageen moss, buttermilk-cream, skimmed milk and some flour. I particularly admired the way that some of the cakes had been decorated with sweets obtained as gifts from shops in St Peter Port.

When the meal was over and the tables cleared away, music and songs filled the hall and in fact an afternoon of fun was enjoyed by all taking the minds off all thoughts generated by the awful war being waged and of our position in it.

We continued to organise the same kind of treat each year even after Mr Tetley had been sent to Germany because of his nationality. He had left a considerable sum of money in my care to continue Christmas treats and also to help in organising a Children's Soup Kitchen at Cobo.

However, in the last year of the Occupation it was felt that it would be unfair to beg for help from people who had so little for their own families. However the Soup Kitchen functioned for the period of increasing difficulty continuing to the very end of the Occupation.

Method by which meal was cooked

204

Guernsey French Poem
J'n'iron pus a La Maire!
(Chanson St Martinaise) — Metivier

L'soleil fait L'amour à la terre,
    L'cieil est doux, l'air sérain;
A Saint la maire est coum ùn verre,
    A'bat déjà sen pillain;
L'voûs, car il est haut temps, Jean, Pierre,
    Marguerite et Mad'lon!
Not' fortune est dans not' galere,
    A'va coum un mouisson!
Quand les houmards, sangllottànt d'fret,
    S'hébergeront sus l's âtres,
Quànd l's ormers grimp'ront sus l'Béquet,
    J'n'iron pus ès banâtres,
        Es banâtres,
    J'n'iron pus ès banâtres!

Blûe, ou verte coum' de la plise;
    L'cher mireux du soleil,
Qu'l'ique rouane ou rouablle nère ou grise,
    Que l'temps seit laid ou bel —
Blànc coum' la née où l'berouet joue.
    M'nichànt quiq'malin caoup,
J'navique et j'ris, parmi la broue,
    De Roc-Dovre a Lihaou!
Quand les Fràncais f'ront virair d'bord
    Nos murs de coeur de quêne,
Quand j'haiss'teron leux tricolor,
    J'n'iron pus à la sênne,
        A la sênne,
J'n'iron pus a là sênne!

L'etat du terrien m'piaît guère,
    Car il est triste adret, —
Baillies-mé nos rocquers pour douaire,
    Pour demeure un baté!
Baillies-me l'camp ou la querue
    Jamais n'tourne motté!

205

Baillies-mé l'turbot, la mouarue,
    La sole et l'gris mulet!
Auve les vèles en berdelle ès mâts,
    Si j'ronfilon dans la câle,
Quand les dravàns craindront les vracs,
    J'n'iron pus à la tralle!
        A la tralle,
    J'n'iron pus à la tralle!

L'jour creit fai-d'ver l'vent suffle et crie,
    Il enffe not' can' vas!
V'la Pierre et Jean sus la cauchie,
    Éfànts à vot' travas!
Ah! vou r'viendraiz brâment, vos quatre,
    Soupair, fiers et goguets,
D'vànt not' raguer, les pids sus l'ârtre,
    Chàntant coum' des coquets!
Quànd not' soleil àira perdu
Sa lueur brillànte et claire,
Quànd j's'ron tous à la gar de Gu,
    J'n'iron pus à la maire,
    A la maire,
    J'n'iron pus à la maire!

Guernsey French Poem
We will go no more to sea
Poem Relating to St Martin's
Translation by P. J. Girard

The sun makes love to the Earth,
The sky is calm, the air serene;
At Saints the sea is like glass,
The tide is full;
Get up because it is already late, Jean, Pierre,
Marguerite and Mad'lon,
Our fortune is in our boat,
It goes like a bird!
When the lobsters shivering with cold,
Will take refuge on the hearths,

When the ormers climb on Becquet,
We will no longer work our crab-pots
   Work our crab-pots,
We will no longer work our crab-pots.

Blue or green as eel-grass,
The dear mirror of the sun,
May the water black or grey, scolds or grumbles,
May the weather be fair or foul,
White as snow, where the foam plays,
Boding some cunning blow,
I sail and I laugh amid the spume,
From Roches Douvres to Lihou!
When the French will cause to put about,
Our walls of heart of oak,
When we hoist their tricolour,
We will no longer go a seining,
   A seining,
We will no longer go a seining.

The life of a farmer tempts me not at all,
As he is really very wretched,
Give me our rocks for my dower,
A boat for a home!
Give me that field where the plough
Never turns a clod!
Give me the turbot, the cod,
The sole and the grey mullet!
With the sails in shreds around the masts,
If we snore in the hold,
When the skate will fear the rock fish,
We will no longer go a trawling,
   A trawling,
We will no longer go a trawling.

The dawn breaks, hasten, the wind whistles and shrieks,
It swells our canvas,
There is Pierre and Jean on the pier,
Children, to your work!
You will come back safely, all four
To supper, happy and gay,
Before our blaze, your feet on the hearth,

Singing like cockerels,
When our sun will have lost
Its bright, clear light,
When we will all be in God's care,
We will go no more to sea,
    To sea,
We will go no more to sea.

Local terminology involving tenure of land and local administration

Camp: Strip of land into which large Open Fields were divided, e.g. Camp du Moulin. This was a 'camp' situated near to the Sausmarez Mill and in the Open Field of St Martin's.

Open fields: This refers to large fields unfenced and divided into strips called 'camps' held and cultivated by many different farmers.

Courtil: Field.

Trepy: Megalithic Tomb.

Lande: Land not suitable for remunerative cultivation.

Butière: A strip of unploughed land at the end of a field used as a turning area for the plough especially when a heavy wooden framed plough was used, pulled by a team of oxen and horses as at La Grande Tcherue.

La Grande Tcherue: With the introduction of the large wooden plough community ploughing became the rule. The ploughs were drawn by teams of oxen supplemented by horses belonging to neighbouring farmers. The result favoured the culture of parsnips because of the depth of soil turned over by the plough. La Grande Tcherue was usually celebrated by suppers of Guernsey gâche and other delicacies whilst Guernsey songs ended the day. The farms in a neighbourhood in turn used La Grande Tcherue and the neighbours usually turned up to help even if they just had a spade or a strong wooden mallet to break the clods of earth.

Jaonnière: This was a furzebrake providing bracken-fern for the floor of the sleeping quarters of the animals as well as gorse which was very much in demand for bakers' ovens as well as those of the population.

Feugré: This word describes a furze and bracken-brake.

Menage: This word was used to describe a house — especially a farmhouse as well as its immediate surroundings.

Haugard: This was the name used for a stack-yard.

Le Haugard with Pilotins.

La Batterie: The name of the machine used to thresh corn as well as to describe the jollifications among the neighbours who had assembled to help the farmer concerned to thresh his corn.

Corvée: Forced Labour which was used in Feudal times.

Poulage: Two fowls a year per house were payable by tenants to the Lord of the Manor or 'Seigneur' of the Feudal Fief involved.

Livre de Perchage: This was meant to act as a register of all the tenants on a particular fief. Formerly it was usual to revise the register every twenty years. The revision was carried out by twelve tenants sworn as a douzaine by the Royal Court.

Masse: This was the name given to the base of a Windmill.

Saisie: To seize or arrest chattels to try to compel people to pay money due.

Tertre: This word defines a hillock.

Croix: In Roman Catholic days among other places Crosses were erected along the paths used by parishioners to reach their Parish Church. Thus 'La Croix des Goddards', 'La Croix de St Germain', 'Le Croix de St George', 'La Croix

210

Nicolle', 'La Croix des Landelles' all marked one of the paths to the Castel Church.

Other church paths existed to lead parishioners to the Parish Church. But all the Crosses of this kind were destroyed when the Calvinists took over all the religious responsibilities of the Island.

Audience de Paroisse

Through the medieval period and up to 1608 it was the custom that the conveyance following the sale of property should be carried out in two stages. The first one was carried out between the parties concerned in the entrance of the Parish Church in the hearing of the parishioners present.

The second stage appears to have been more formal when the details of the transactions involved were disclosed before two or more Jurats of the Royal Court in order to formalise the transaction.

During the long period in which this practice was in use it is not perfectly clear whether the matter was always finalised within the precincts of the Royal Court. It is thought possible that the Jurats may have at times visited the Church.

Menhir at Le Crocq, St Saviour's.

Menhir: A mysterious addition to certain areas was a tall upright mass of stone called a Menhir.

The best known of such erections can still be seen at Les Paysans in St Pierre du Bois and is called 'La Longue Roque'. Viewed from the correct position the menhir appears to provide one with what appears to be the profile of a woman. This could have been associated with the earth mother — but who knows.

Two others can be seen at Le Crocq, St Saviour's, both in an area which was once considered to be agricultural and records also exist which refer to such menhirs which have now disappeared, e.g. In the Castel Parish the existence of the following menhirs is recorded: 'La Rocque à Boeuf' and 'La Longue Pierre'.

Clos: This refers to a piece of land usually situated near a farmer's residence. It was cut off from surroundings by dry stone walls or thick Guernsey hedges. Probably used for stock. Definitely used in 1470, possibly earlier.

Fries: This name is used to describe pasture land.

Congé: This was a levy or permit or triezeième paid by the purchaser of realty to the Seigneur of his fief when property changed hands.

In 1979 the States approved the cancellation of the existing system concerning the payment of Congé but the assembly approved the annual payment of £50,000 a year, for five years to be divided among the Seigneurs by way of compensation. After this any income from Congé would accrue to the Crown along with the income from the Crown Fiefs themselves. Actually by virtue of a decision of 1947 this Crown income continued to be relinquished by the Crown in favour of the States.

Fief: The origin of the word is not known but the Feudal System came to us from the Continent and it was based on a principle which can be defined as the holding of land implying duties to be discharged by the holder which would benefit the owner — 'Le Seigneur' and different from the idea of land being used solely as an investment. This admitted considerable variations from Fief to Fief in the conditions attached to the holdings.

212

Assembly of the Fief Beuval in front garden of house at Les Sages.

Bouvées: Bouvée was the name given to a conveniently sized feudal holding which originally was supposed to represent the area that could be ploughed by a team of oxen in a year.

Meetings of Fiefs: These meetings were at one time held very regularly but unfortunately the reverse is now the rule as the Seigneurs have found that with the fall in value of money and the sub-division of properties their dues are not worth collecting.

It would appear that whilst the Seigneur or his representative attended a Court meeting it was the *Seneschal* who presided and received the assistance of the *Vavasseurs* in deciding matters in dispute between Seigneur and tenant.

The *Greffier* acted as the clerk of the Court and recorded the names and properties of those who had become tenants since the last court day, etc.

The *Prévôt's* duty was to execute the orders of the Court and to prosecute non-payers.

The *Sergeant* maintained order and assisted the Prévôt in his duties. The office of *Grenetier* was given to a tenant who was empowered to receive dues which were often paid in kind.

Pilotins: This is the word used to describe the 'stone mushrooms' and platforms on which tall ricks of straw were

213

Seal of the Fief St Michel.

held until threshing time arrived when the grain was separated from the straw.

Raising the corn well up from the ground protected it from the attention of rats and mice. In addition the raising up of the stack enabled a current of air to circulate below it so that mould, etc., was kept out.

Prai: Name given to a water-meadow.

Pieche: Portion of land in a large field which had no hedges as in early days — or could be part of a large field in modern times, e.g. 'Enne pieche de brocolus'. A cauliflower patch — such a 'pieche' in modern days would normally be in a field enclosed by hedges.

Parque: Pigsty, specially built to house pigs.

Parquet: The name of a structure able to house animals such as rams.

214

Messier: Name given to a man responsible for catching and housing wandering or straying animals. This was especially important during *Mession* which was the period when crops were growing fast in the 'Open Fields'. *Messieres* — Place where animals could be kept until owner was discovered.

Banon: The period when the harvest was safely gathered into the farms and the Open Fields were available for grazing. The approximate dates when Banon was in operation was from September to March.

Officials of Fief Beuval.

OTHER GUERNSEY PRESS PUBLICATIONS

ALDERNEY — *by Victor Coysh*

BAILIWICK BASTIONS — The fortifications of the Bailiwick
of Guernsey — *by L. James Marr*

CALL OF THE ISLAND — Guernsey Remembered — *by Victor Coysh*

CHANNEL ISLETS — The Lesser Channel Islands — *by Victor Coysh*

COUNTRY BY THE SEA — Cliff Walks in Guernsey
(four volumes: Routes 1-4) — *by Carel Toms*

EXPLORE HERM — *by Alan Barber*

EXPLORE SARK — *by Alan Barber*

THE GERMAN OCCUPATION OF THE CHANNEL ISLANDS —
The Official History of the Occupation Years
by Charles Cruickshank

GUERNSEY AS IT WAS — A nostalgic record of life
at the turn of the century — *by Nick Machon*

MORE GUERNSEY AS IT WAS — *by Nick Machon*

HERM, ITS MYSTERIES & CHARM — *by Michael Marshall*

100 YEARS OF PUBLIC TRANSPORT — A short history of the
Guernsey Railway Co. Ltd. — *by W. J. Carman*

THE ISLAND OF GUERNSEY — A full colour picture book
of Guernsey — *by Robin Millard*

ISLANDERS IN KITBAGS — Men and women who fought for the
Liberation — *by Richard Allisette*

ISLANDS IN FOCUS — An aerial appreciation of the Bailiwick
of Guernsey — *by Brian Green*

LIBERATION! — The Story of Guernsey in Captivity and the Long
Road to Freedom — *by Nick Machon*

A BRIEF GUIDE TO LIHOU ISLAND — *by Robin Borwick*

LIHOU ISLAND, NEVER AT HALF MOON — *by Robin Borwick*

THE LONG GOODBYE — A Guernseywoman's Story of the
Evacuation Years — *by Olive Quin*

THE LOVE APPLE — 101 Tomato Recipes — *by Georgina Keen*

MAYDAY! MAYDAY! — A History of the Guernsey Lifeboat
Station — *by Guy Blampied*

MYSTERIOUS MOUND — How the world's oldest stone building
was unearthed at Les Fouaillages, on Guernsey's L'Ancresse
Common — *by Nick Machon*

ON THE EDGE OF SARK — *by Des Lyver*

SARK — A History of Sark — *by Ken Hawkes*

TOILERS OF THE SEA — *by Victor Hugo*

UNEVEN KEEL — *by Malcolm Robson*

WALKING ABOUT ST PETER PORT — Route One — *by Carel Toms*

WALKING ABOUT ST PETER PORT — Route Two — *by Carel Toms*

WALKS WITH A CAR IN GUERNSEY — *by Alan Barber*

WALKS WITH A MEAL IN GUERNSEY — *by Alan Barber*

25 YEARS OF BISH BANJO — *by Barbara Faye*

The family of islands centred around Guernsey has
lived under the constant threat of invasion from neighbours.

As a consequence, fortification of a scale gigantic
for so small an area became essential.

L. James Marr's intriguing book seeks to pinpoint
the locations of and provide the background stories to
these various military works.

ISBN 0 902550 11 X

A GUERNSEY PRESS PUBLICATION

Channel Islets is a book with a difference, for nothing has been published quite like it before.

While several of these 'lesser isles' have been featured in local publications never have they been detailed so appealingly.

In addition to their history and topography, the author explains how the islands may be reached and lists most of the outstanding Channel Islands rocks.

With the added help of Carel Toms' illustrations, Victor Coysh has produced a gem that will be of interest to both islander and visitor alike.

ISBN   0   902550   12   8

A GUERNSEY PRESS PUBLICATION

This is the official history of the German occupation of the Channel Islands, based on British War Cabinet, Foreign Office, Admiralty, War Office, Air Ministry, and Home Office papers in the Public Record Office; SHAEF papers; German Foreign Ministry and Wehrmacht records; files left by Feldkommandandtur in Guernsey and Jersey; and the Channel Islands' own wartime papers.

ISBN   0 902550 02 0

A GUERNSEY PRESS PUBLICATION